EAT MOR CHIKIN®

INSPIRE MORE PEOPLE

S. TRUETT CATHY

EAT MOR CHIKIN: INSPIRE MORE PEOPLE
Copyright © 2002 Chick-fil-A, Inc.

Written in collaboration with Dick Parker
Published by Looking Glass Books
Decatur, Georgia

Manufactured in the United States of America
Printed on recycled paper
ISBN 1-929619-08-1

Partial listing of trademarks[1] and products of Chick-fil-A, Inc. and its affiliates

Chick-fil-A®	First 'N Best®
The Dwarf House® [2]	Cool Wrap®
Truett's Grill® [3]	Chick-fil-A Spicy Chicken Cool Wraps®
Chick-fil-A® Express	Chick-fil-A Chicken Caesar Cool Wraps®
Chick-fil-A® Chicken Sandwich	Chick-fil-A Chargrilled Chicken Cool Wraps®
Chick-fil-A® Chicken Salad Sandwich	
Chick-fil-A® Chicken Biscuit	We Didn't Invent The Chicken, Just The Chicken Sandwich®
Chick-fil-A® Chargrilled Chicken Sandwich	Eat Mor Chikin®
Chick-fil-A® Chargrilled Chicken Deluxe Sandwich	Growing Kids Inside and Out®
Chick-fil-A® Chargrilled Chicken Club Sandwich	Chick-fil-A.M.®
	Chick-fil-A® Catering Great Taste
Chick-fil-A® Chargrilled Chicken Garden Salad	Chick-fil-A® Kid's Meal
Chick-fil-A® Nuggets	Chick-fil-A Charity Championship® hosted by Nancy Lopez
Chick-fil-A Waffle Potato Fries®	Camp WinShape® [4]
Chick-fil-A Chick-n-Strips®	WinShape Centre® [4]
Chick-fil-A Chick-n-Strips® Salad	WinShape Homes® [4]
Icedream®	WinShape Wilderness® [4]

1. Unless otherwise noted herein, all trademarks are owned by CFA Properties, Inc., and licensed to Chick-fil-A, Inc.

2. A registered trademark of Dwarf House, Inc.

3. A registered trademark of HJG Dwarf House, Inc.

4. A registered trademark of WinShape Centre, Inc.

EAT MOR CHIKIN®

INSPIRE MORE PEOPLE

Foreword

FREDERICK F. REICHHELD
Author of
The Loyalty Effect: The Hidden Force Behind Growth, Profits, and Lasting Value
and
Loyalty Rules! How Today's Leaders Build Lasting Relationships

To be perfectly honest, I was unfamiliar with Truett Cathy or Chick-fil-A when I wrote my first *Harvard Business Review* article about business loyalty in 1989. Now, two books and five HBR articles on the subject later, I can't imagine a serious discussion of loyalty in business that does not reference the accomplishments of the Cathy family and their company. Thank goodness a friend of mine read that first article and insisted that I get to know this remarkable family and their remarkable company. Why? Because Chick-fil-A has succeeded by designing its entire business system around customer loyalty; because Truett Cathy recognizes that a company earns customers' loyalty by consistently delivering superior value; because Chick-fil-A has created a degree of loyalty among its customers, employees, and restaurant franchise Operators that I had never imagined possible, particularly in the quick-serve restaurant business.

Customer loyalty to an organization is a direct result of loyalty within that organization. Truett Cathy's loyalty to Chick-fil-A restaurant Operators is evident in the selection process. "We don't select or even seriously consider an Operator unless we want the individual to be with us until one of us dies or retires," he says.

I surveyed several Chick-fil-A restaurant Operators to find out what could possibly make them want to stay with the same restaurant business for an average of twenty years. I learned that they stayed because: 1) they are proud of their association with

Truett Cathy, 2) they believe in the philosophy that guides Chick-fil-A, and 3) they can earn two to three times as much income owning a Chick-fil-A restaurant for little up-front investment than they can managing a restaurant at the competition or most other retailers. I was immediately skeptical. Fast food is an extremely price-sensitive industry, and I could not imagine such a generous franchise agreement while still earning sufficient profits to grow a company to the scale of Chick-fil-A. I knew it costs at least $1 million to build a free-standing restaurant and that Truett Cathy was building about sixty of these per year. He managed to do this while remaining a private company, so the company's cash flow had to provide the foundation for this expansion.

The deeper I dug into the economics of Chick-fil-A, the more amazed I became. Chick-fil-A's same-store sales and total percentage growth were growing faster than the industry king-pins such as McDonald's and Burger King, despite Chick-fil-A's advertising expenditures of 2 to 3 percent of sales compared to more than 6 percent of sales at the big brands. Even more amazing was the fact that Chick-fil-A units achieved higher sales per square foot than McDonald's et al. despite the fact that Chick-fil-A stays closed on Sundays, one of the biggest sales days for restaurants.

I finally came to realize that the accounting and economics I had learned at The Harvard Business School was flawed, flawed because their arithmetic did not capture the powerful advantages of loyal relationships. This loyalty effect, the full range of economic and human benefits that accrue to leaders who treat their customers, Operators, and employees in a manner worthy of their loyalty, is at the core of most of the truly successful growth companies in the world today. And there is no clearer case study of the loyalty effect than Chick-fil-A.

Consider the fact that Chick-fil-A has never had to issue stock in order to finance the creation of more than 1,000 restaurants across America. Consider the fact that the company has grown to over $1.25 billion in sales. Consider further, that the firm's core economics are so strong that management hopes to more than triple sales over the next decade, while at the same time pay down all outstanding debt. To anyone knowledgeable in the quick-serve restaurant business, this kind of cash generation is a miracle—especially given the outstanding financial return for the chain's restaurant Operators. This cash generation is even more noteworthy when one considers that Chick-fil-A provides $1 million in annual college scholarships, and in addition, the firm allocates funds to other charities to support foster care homes, summer camps for children, and several ministries.

In my most recent book, *Loyalty Rules!: How Today's Leaders Build Lasting Relationships*, I have compared the miracle at Chick-fil-A to similarly miraculous companies such as Enterprise Rent-a-Car, Vanguard, Northwestern Mutual Insurance, Cisco, Intuit, Dell Computer, Southwest Airlines, and Harley-Davidson. What I found was that each of these companies is guided by a leadership philosophy that is focused on building mutually beneficial relationships—and that the key to these firms' success is a leadership team who understands how to put these principles into practice.

This book by Truett Cathy reveals and clarifies that philosophy of loyalty. His stories will help you understand how that philosophy has guided his life, his family, and his leadership team. They will help you to see how you can put the principles of loyalty into practice in your own relationships. Most importantly, they should give you confidence that when leaders put the welfare of others first, there is no limit to what they can accomplish. By building relationships worthy of trust and commitment, leaders can fundamentally transform the economics of a business—and the lives of those people it touches. By focusing on helping others around him make the most of their lives, Truett Cathy has achieved outstanding success of his own. Follow his example and you can do the same.

Preface

Driven by intensity and purpose, Truett Cathy begins each day with the excitement and anticipation of a child awakening on Christmas morning. Giving in to personal weariness, fatigue, or frustration is simply not an option for him.

In Truett's mind, there is always a way to get the job done. "Never give up," he will say. "There is some solution for every problem if you explore all possibilities."

Resolute in his values, which are based on biblical principles, he never gives in to moral compromise. Though kind and generous to all, he remains firm and determined.

His story will encourage you to look deeper, go further, and try harder.

—MARGARET W. CARTER
Longtime Administrative Assistant
to Truett Cathy and wife of Dr. Charles Q.
Carter, the Cathys' pastor

EAT MOR CHIKIN®

INSPIRE MORE PEOPLE

Chapter One

Unexpected Opportunities

Put two Cows on a billboard with a bucket of paint and a brush, and they'll create some unexpected opportunities. In 1995 we gave the Cows responsibility for taking the message of Chick-fil-A to the public. From their perch high above the highway, and now on radio and television, they remind people in their unique style to "Eat Mor Chikin!" The Cows still haven't learned to spell, and their grammar leaves a lot to be desired, but the opportunities are real. Five years after they painted their first billboard, Chick-fil-A had doubled our sales volume, achieving annual sales of more than $1 billion.

The lesson from the Cows is the lesson of my life: Take advantage of unexpected opportunities. We had not planned a major billboard campaign, but the Cows created so much buzz when they appeared, we realized they were presenting a special opportunity to increase awareness of Chick-fil-A and have fun at the same time.

Above: The Chick-fil-A Cows have created tremendous awareness for us and at the same time led to unexpected opportunities.

The history of Chick-fil-A, in fact, is a series of unexpected opportunities. When we responded to them, we often found ourselves richly blessed.

The Chick-fil-A Chicken Sandwich itself was born in the wake of an unexpected opportunity. When one of my first two restaurants burned to the ground, I found myself with time on my hands and the availability to develop a new recipe.

The boom in mall development in the 1970s and '80s gave Chick-fil-A the opportunity to expand our business quickly while minimizing real estate costs and identifying ourselves with a quality shopping experience.

Chick-fil-A Kids Meals offered us the opportunity to influence children with a prize that carried with it a positive message.

A chance encounter with a teenage boy who had lost his parents led to opportunities that have resulted in the establishment of the Chick-fil-A WinShape Centre Foundation, which supports foster homes, summer camps, and college scholarships, touching the lives of thousands of children and young adults— and literally saving some of them.

The lesson that is continually reinforced in me is that to take advantage of unexpected opportunities, we must leave ourselves available. If we had set lofty long-range goals for our company's growth, our capital might have been so tied up in construction that we would have been unable to respond to these opportunities.

Many successful people I know set magnificent goals for themselves, then let nothing stand in the way of their achievement. I don't engage in that kind of long-range planning. Instead, I leave myself and my company available to take advantage of opportunities as they arise.

I'm not suggesting that we wander aimlessly waiting for opportunities to drop out of the sky. We commit ourselves to a purpose, and we don't overcommit our resources. That way of thinking has allowed us to grow steadily into a billion-dollar business with 1,000 restaurants while responding to the needs of people around us.

MANY OF THE UNEXPECTED OPPORTUNITIES WE ENCOUNTER are small but significant. On a Saturday morning I was showing a visitor some of the landmarks near our home south of Atlanta. We stopped at the Lovejoy Station Chick-fil-A restaurant and found a birthday party in progress. A three-year-old girl was surrounded by her parents, aunts, uncles, friends, and two older cousins dressed up as Veggie Tales characters. It was my first unexpected opportunity of the day. I grabbed a handful of plush toy Cows—miniature versions of our famous Chick-fil-A billboard characters—and held one out for the little girl.

"What do the Cows say?" I asked.

She looked at me, puzzled. (Remember, she was barely three.)

"What do the Cows say?" I repeated.

"Moo," she replied.

Everyone laughed at her pretty good answer, and I gave her a Cow and a hug and whispered the real answer to her. Then I turned to her mother and asked, "What do the Cows say?"

"Eat more chicken!" her mother cried.

"Yea!" I said, and I gave her an *Eat Mor Chikin* Cow as everyone in the restaurant laughed with us.

Then, one by one, each person quoted the Cows and laughed. I gave away most of the Cows, and we all made some special memories that they will associate with Chick-fil-A.

I enjoy few things more than making people—especially children—smile. The Cows do the trick almost every time.

In the middle of the same afternoon my friend and I drove to Truett's Grill, a restaurant we opened in 1996 to commemorate my fiftieth year in the restaurant business. (I like to tell people that the 1996 Summer Olympic Games were held in Atlanta as part of our celebration.) Truett's Grill is a 1950s-style diner spilling over with atmosphere. A rotating neon sign out front gives customers their first clue that they're about to take a nostalgic ride, and the vintage cars parked out front reinforce that message.

We stepped inside Truett's Grill at about 3 P.M., and the place was alive with the energy of young people. I guess kids of every generation are drawn to a diner. People were waiting to get tables, so we took a pair of stools at the counter and ordered milkshakes. I struck up a conversation with a group of a dozen teenagers who were sitting at nearby booths and several stools around us. They were from a church in Griffin, Georgia, and had been working all day to fix up a house for an elderly couple. Their smiles and laughter made it clear that they had enjoyed devoting themselves to the well-being of others, and their devotion was another reminder to me of the promise of the coming generation. I wanted them to know that I appreciated what they had done, so I gave each of them a "Be Our Guest" card for a free Chick-fil-A Chicken Sandwich. Another unexpected opportunity.

Small Cows and free sandwiches are my tokens of appreciation, and people seem to enjoy receiving them.

THE UNEXPECTED OPPORTUNITY I ENJOY MOST is the opportunity to turn a frown into a smile. Many of my unexpected opportunities occur on airplanes. One afternoon I was sitting on a plane as it waited . . . and waited . . . to roll away from the gate for takeoff. The delay continued for over an hour, until finally the captain announced that our plane was broken and another one had been called in to take us to our destination. The passengers groaned. The captain then announced that "Truett Cathy, founder of Chick-fil-A" was on board, waiting with the rest of them. I asked the flight attendant if I could hand out "Be Our Guest" cards to the passengers; I had a stack in my pocket (as I always do), enough for everybody on the plane. Passengers up and down the aisle smiled, and several told me it wasn't such a bad day after all.

On another plane a man recognized me and sat in the empty seat beside me. He introduced himself and said he was aware of Chick-fil-A and some of the principles we uphold. Before he moved to his assigned seat, he wondered if I might be able to advise him on a matter that was troubling him.

He had two children, a fifteen-year-old son and a seventeen-year-old daughter, and he was worried about the many temptations they were facing with drugs, alcohol, sex, and inappropriate friends. The man had ordered a beer from the flight attendant, and I thought about the inconsistency in his concerns and his action. I didn't want to turn him off by coming across as pious, but I did want to illustrate the point.

"Do you encourage your son and daughter to drink beer?" I asked.

"No, I don't," he said.

I looked down, and then he looked down at the beer in his hand. I didn't say anything more to him about it. He got up and moved to his seat before the plane took off.

We have an impact on our children by what we say, but

particularly by what we do. They forget many of the things we say, but they observe everything we do. We can't expect to keep beer in the refrigerator and expect our fifteen-year-old not to drink beer. These are the unexpected opportunities parents receive every day—opportunities to influence their children positively by their actions. When the plane landed and I stood to leave, the man came up and thanked me for what I had said.

A WOMAN CALLED SOME YEARS AGO AND ASKED, "Do you remember the dwarf that sat in your restaurant?"

"Yes," I said.

"Well, I know who has it."

She was referring to a little statue of a dwarf that stood in the Dwarf House, my first restaurant, for several years but had been stolen about the same time a little sign over the "dwarf door" out front was stolen. I had posted a sign offering a twenty-five-dollar reward for the return of the dwarf, but after more than a decade it was still missing. I always assumed some teenage pranksters had taken it one night on a dare while they were in the restaurant.

The woman on the telephone continued, "My father and I have looked at that dwarf for years, and we're trying to persuade my brother to bring it back. We should have made him return it years ago."

I knew then that the woman's brother had been the teenage thief, and the dwarf had been sitting in his bedroom ever since.

"We never told him to bring it back," she said. "Now he's getting out of prison for stealing a car, and we know that if we had insisted that he do the right thing a long time ago, he might not have stolen that car."

As it turned out, the dwarf thief had a partner in crime who had taken the sign, and likewise had grown up to become a criminal and serve time in prison. He called me on the telephone and said he had become a Christian while in prison. Upon his release, he was going through some things in his garage and came across our sign. He brought it back and apologized, saying he wanted to make things right.

"And you remember that dwarf that was stolen?" he asked.

"Yes," I said. "Somebody recently called and said her brother had it."

"Well, I know who he is, and I'm going to talk to him."

A few days later a man came in carrying the dwarf. He was followed by his three little girls.

"Daddy, why are you giving him our dwarf?" the girls asked.

The man made a joke and never apologized for his actions. Like his sister, I wonder what might have happened if she and their father had insisted that the boy do the right thing years earlier. They missed a valuable unexpected opportunity. The statue and the sign are now in our corporate office museum, along with their stories, to remind us to be alert for opportunities.

SOMETIMES I ENJOY CREATING UNEXPECTED OPPORTUNITIES for others. I was mentoring a young man who lived in Birmingham, Alabama. He needed a car, and I wanted to help him. More than the car, though, he needed direction. I sent him a series of sermon tapes by Dr. Charles Stanley, pastor at First Baptist Church in Atlanta, and asked him to listen to them. My hope was that we could discuss some of Dr. Stanley's messages, and my friend would grow spiritually.

As a reward for listening to the tapes, I was going to give him the car he wanted. But I didn't tell him that. Rather, on the last sermon tape I recorded my own message over Dr. Stanley's words, telling my friend that the keys to his car were waiting for him in Atlanta.

Over the next few weeks I called my friend periodically, asking him about the progress he had made listening to the tapes. Each time he promised to get started listening soon, but with his busy schedule he had not gotten around to it.

After more than a month, it became apparent that he was not going to listen to the tapes, and I suggested that he bring them back to me. While he sat in my office, we listened to the last tape together, both of us terribly sad because of his missed opportunity.

It was a powerful lesson—one that neither he nor I will forget. To receive a blessing, we often have to take action first.

Sometimes a bad situation can turn into an unexpected opportunity. Some years ago I bought an older house on a large lot in College Park, Georgia, and had it remodeled so we could use it as our second foster home. When it came time to have the property rezoned, however, the neighbors adamantly opposed our efforts. They didn't want our children living in their neighborhood. They didn't believe us when we told them about the caliber of our program and the dedication of our children to overcoming their circumstances. The zoning board, and eventually the entire Fulton County Commission, acceded to the will of the neighbors, and we were blocked from using the house for a foster home.

About that time I learned that a nice boy in the Sunday

school class I taught had seven siblings and was living with his parents in a three-bedroom, one-bathroom home. The father sold cleaning supplies; the mother home-schooled the children and took in sewing for extra income. They were working hard and dedicating themselves to their children, but they likely would never afford a larger home.

The opportunity appeared obvious. I made some discreet inquiries to make sure that the family would not be offended or embarrassed if I offered to swap houses with them. (It takes both a gracious receiver and giver to make the gift work.) The family now lives in a house appropriate to their size.

You may have noticed a pattern to these unexpected opportunities. Most of them are opportunities to give. Nearly every moment of every day we have the opportunity to give something to someone else—our time, our love, or our resources. I have always found more joy in giving when I did not expect anything in return. That's why I'm so thankful that the Lord brought foster children into my life—truly needy individuals who need love more than money, and who appreciate smiles and hugs as much as popcorn and ice cream.

Unexpected opportunities almost always carry with them the chance to be a faithful steward and to influence others positively. These were the lessons I began to learn in childhood from my mother, my siblings, and others around me who cared enough to teach me.

We change the world, and ourselves, by our response to unexpected opportunities. How will you respond today?

CHAPTER TWO

How Firm a Foundation

A man from Eatonton, Georgia, which lies about halfway between Atlanta and Augusta, called awhile back and asked if I wanted to buy the little house I was born in over eighty years ago. I drove over to look at it and consider his proposition. I decided against buying the house, but as the man took me through it a few hazy memories came to mind: the vague recollection of a smokehouse, a time when I was sitting in a horse-drawn wagon, and a stack of firewood. I was only three years old when my nearly destitute parents abandoned the rural life for better opportunities in Atlanta, so my experiences in Eatonton were limited.

It was in that house that I drew my first breath. My parents named me after George W. Truett, the great preacher and evangelist of the first half of the twentieth century, for whom the theological seminary at Baylor University is named.

My family couldn't afford doctors and hospitals, so when it came time for my mother to deliver, a midwife came and as-

Above: The Cathy family home in Eatonton, Georgia.

sisted. In fact, the first time I saw a doctor was after I went into the army. If I or any of my brothers or sisters got a cut or a sore throat, Mother took care of us as best she could.

In those days before modern medicine, her limited arsenal was sometimes overwhelmed. She could not stop polio from attacking my sister Esther before her first birthday, confining her to leg braces and crutches, and later a wheelchair. And when my six-year-old brother J.G. was playing outside and a stick jabbed him deep in the stomach, my mother had no antibiotics to stop the ensuing peritonitis that would soon kill him. That was before I was born, so I never knew J.G. But Esther often talked about what a sweet, lovable boy he was, and what a great loss his passing was to our family.

Rural life left many scars. Six years before I was born, a fire destroyed the family home and all its contents. Neighbors pitched in where they could, replacing clothes and toys, and the home was rebuilt. But with no insurance, the expense laid a heavy financial burden on the family. Esther later recalled hearing our father speak with pride about his success as a farmer—his corn and cotton, cattle, swine, and honeybees. But he did not have enough money to have her polio treated without help from Scottish Rite Hospital.

He deepened his involvement in real estate after World War I, as land speculators drove up prices. But soon after I was born in 1921, boll weevils appeared in the fields around Eatonton, and my father quickly went broke. Land wasn't worth the taxes people owed on it, and we owned nothing of value. Rather than perish, we moved to Atlanta, and my dad got a job with the Life and Casualty Insurance Company of Nashville, selling policies and collecting premiums. He earned so little money, however, my mother had to step in and become the family breadwinner.

Every morning Dad drove off in his old Model-T Ford to collect insurance premiums from customers scattered all over. On cold mornings when I was a little older, he told me to go out and crank the car for him. That meant pouring hot water into the radiator (antifreeze had not been invented, so we drained the radiator on cold nights), laying hot towels on the manifold, then turning the hand crank on the front of the car. Mom packed Dad a lunch of sausage biscuits and fried pies, and he drove off with his corn cob pipe in his mouth to see his customers. At midday he would stop somewhere along the way, buy some milk from a farmer, and sit under a shade tree to eat.

By that time the Depression had the world in its grip, and many of Dad's customers couldn't afford the insurance he had sold them. Premiums were anywhere from a dime to a dollar a week—money many people didn't have. So they paid their premiums with merchandise from the farm. Dad would come home with eggs, chickens, country ham, sorghum syrup, or flour. That was his financial contribution to the family.

The problem with that system was that every Friday the premiums still had to be paid to the company. On Thursday nights I would help Dad prepare a report showing how much money he had collected. From the collections he was supposed to take out his commission and send the balance to Nashville.

"How much did we collect this week?" he would ask me.

"Sixty dollars," I would reply.

"That can't be right. The company says I owe them seventy-five."

So we would go through the figures again and come up with the same sad result, and instead of adding to the family cash flow, my father would borrow from it to pay the premiums.

I never knew the father my sister described—a man realizing his dreams and making a decent living on the farm. The Depression changed him—took the life out of him.

Some weeks were profitable, but after Dad paid for gasoline and repairs on the car, rarely was anything left. His failure as a businessman was not for lack of hard work or desire to achieve. He would drive five miles to collect a twenty-five-cent premium. But he failed nonetheless—as millions did during the Depression.

My mother then began taking boarders in our rented home in the West End section of Atlanta. For a dollar a day a boarder got a bed—we put two or three beds in each bedroom—and two meals a day. We had only one bathroom, so the boarders had to schedule around each other. Our family, of course, got the bathroom last, with the children bringing up the rear. My two brothers, four sisters, and I took our baths on Saturday.

Rearing seven children and running a boarding house with seven or eight more people left Mother with no time to relax or to read books. She made all the boarders' beds and kept their rooms straight, cleaned the bathroom, and cooked breakfast and supper for everybody every day, including Sunday dinner.

She spent much of her time in the kitchen, and I spent many days alongside her shucking corn, shelling peas, setting the table, and washing dirty dishes. Almost every night my mother received her reward, compliments on her cooking from the boarders.

Mother never used a recipe. She had an instinct, or an intuition, that guided her through everything she cooked, from fried chicken to sweet potato pie. She salted and peppered her chicken and left it in the ice box all night before she fried it. The next day she fried it in a big iron skillet with a lid. The lid steamed the chicken as it fried, and kept it more moist. Years later I used the same concepts of marinating and cooking when I developed the Chick-fil-A Chicken Sandwich.

As with bathroom privileges, everyone else finished eating before the children took our turns at the table. Then we ate what was left, usually the wings, neck, or feet of a fried chicken. If you've ever seen a big platter of chicken passed around a table, you know that the breast is usually the first to be taken.

For breakfast we ate eggs, or country fried steak, or streak o' lean with hot biscuits and cream gravy. Everything is good if you have hot biscuits and cream gravy to go with it. We took to school what was left from the breakfast table for our lunch—usually biscuits with eggs or streak o' lean. We had an abundance of sorghum syrup, and we'd poke a finger down into the biscuit and pour sorghum in there for a syrup sandwich. I often thought how nice it would be to have a sandwich on loaf bread from the store like other kids I saw.

I monitored how well the family was doing financially by how full the cupboard was. When Dad came home with a twenty-four-pound sack of flour and mother had more groceries than she needed for the day, I understood that to mean things were going well. Just like when we got a full load of coal to burn in the fireplaces. But when Daddy came home with a sack of coal, I knew they didn't have enough money to buy a truckload, and I worried.

The cupboard never went completely bare; the boarders never missed a meal. But the pickings sometimes were dreadfully slim. Mother kept a keg of salted fish in the kitchen and served that for breakfast at least one day a week. During the tightest times, those fish might appear on the table again at supper. Or Mother might take a couple of ten-cent cans of salmon, mix them with some bread crumbs and an egg, and make salmon croquettes.

Mother was a wonderful model of a hard worker—the first person up in the morning and the last down at night. In fact, the only time I ever saw her eyes closed was when she lay in her casket. And the only time I saw her slow down in life was to sit and listen to the "Old Fashioned Revival Hour" from California on the radio every week. That was her devotional time—sitting by the radio and listening to the scripture being read, and to Charles E. Fuller preaching.

Because Mother provided dinner for the boarders at noon on Sunday, she couldn't go to church. But she saw that we children got dressed and off to Sunday school and church.

On Sunday afternoon we might pile into Dad's car and he'd drive us down to McDonough, in Henry County, to visit our aunts and uncles. Dad loved to talk with them about politics— he would talk to anybody about politics. He was sure of his opinions about the New Deal and government assistance programs. In those days families took care of each other. If your mother or brother or cousin needed help, you helped. Our family never reached the point where we asked for welfare, although the day would come when we would need the kind of help President Roosevelt was offering.

On those Sunday afternoons when we stayed at home, I sometimes asked Mother to let me bake a cake. I would find a recipe and follow it carefully, but I often needed something we didn't have, and I would have to either substitute or do without. For instance, I learned to mix baking powder into plain flour to substitute for self-rising flour. The cakes sometimes didn't always turn out like they should with my substitutes, but I learned a lot about cooking, and I enjoyed the trial and error. I also learned to clean up after myself after cooking.

Like any boy, however, I didn't always follow all the rules my mother and father laid out. My parents had their own tools for discipline, castor oil and a leather strap. My mother gave me a dose of castor oil annually, and another one whenever I got careless with my words or attitudes. She prescribed one dose every spring as a preventative, and I sometimes got the druggist to mix the castor oil with cherry drink to mask the horrible flavor.

Then there were the times when I became a little restless, irritable, or non-conforming to the rules, and Mother would say, "What you need is a spring tonic—something to get your thoughts straightened out."

Out came the castor oil from the medicine cabinet—with no cherry drink. It did the trick every time; it would be awhile before I thought about stepping out of line again.

My father was more swift and direct in his discipline. He had a razor strap, and he didn't mind using it on us children if we sassed him in any form or fashion. He had no mercy when it came to punishment, and we tried to avoid it. I was afraid of him. But if I ran from him, I got even more lashes. Mother sometimes tried to intervene, but he wouldn't listen to her.

Looking back, I believe the Depression and Dad's inability to support our family financially affected him deeply. He believed the only way for him to prove his manhood was to rule the roost. We had to do as he said; he left no room for debate.

To people outside our home, Dad must have appeared to be a good husband and father. He was congenial and got along well with most people. I never knew him to cheat on Mom. He seldom used a curse word. He never drank. He was Sunday school superintendent for several years.

But at home he was very hard on us as a family and on me

as a kid. He appeared to take joy in lashing out at Mother with his tongue.

I know now that our situation was not unique. Just because a family is Christian and goes to church and everybody lives under one roof doesn't mean they don't have a lot of problems. I teach Sunday school for thirteen-year-old boys, and each year I ask them, "What one thing would you change in your home if you could?" The answer I hear more than any other is, "I would stop the arguing." Children want to grow up in a peaceful home. When they don't, the consequences can last a lifetime. One boy I visited would not let me into his house because the walls were scarred from where his mother and father threw pots and pans at each other. This boy later ended up in jail.

Because of my family's financial situation, Mother was often on the lookout for a larger house or cheaper rent to keep down our expenses. We moved at least half a dozen times during my childhood, staying primarily on the south side of Atlanta. When a boarder moved out of the house, we immediately put out a sign in the front yard: "Boarder Wanted."

Groceries represented another huge expense that had to be monitored carefully. We ran a charge account at Rogers Grocery at the corner of Oak and Ashby streets—almost everybody did—and Mother paid weekly or monthly, depending on how money was coming in.

A woman who lived on our street generated income by selling cupcakes from her front yard for a nickel, and the few times I had an extra nickel I would buy one from her. I learned fast during the Depression, though, that if I wanted a nickel I would have to earn it. Some people think I'm a penny pincher today, but when you grow up in a family and in a time where every dollar must be stretched as far as it will go, you learn to watch where your money goes.

I was eight years old when I decided it was time for me to earn my own money, so I started selling Coca-Colas door to door. I realized that I could buy six Cokes at the grocery store for a quarter, sell them for a nickel each, and recognize a five-cent profit. That was the beginning of life in the business world for me.

Knocking on people's doors and asking them to buy a Coke from me demanded an awful lot of courage. As a little boy I had a speech impediment so severe I could not pronounce my own name. My mother wrote my name on a card so that if I had to introduce myself to strangers I could let them read it. I remained tongue-tied for years and as a consequence was quite shy. As I grew I had to make myself step out from my timidity. When I got to the point of giving more than 100 public speeches a year, I saw how the Lord took one of my greatest weaknesses—my earlier difficulty in speaking clearly—and used it to magnify His purpose.

The lady who lived across the street from us represented my target market in my Coca-Cola business. Every afternoon she came out onto her front porch and sat in a rocking chair with a Coke in her hand. She and potential customers like her also understood that they could buy six Cokes for a quarter, so I had to offer an incentive for them to buy mine.

One afternoon a neighbor told me, "Truett, we'll buy more Cokes from you if they're iced down."

So I ended my door-to-door sales and built a Coca-Cola stand in the front yard. My mother helped me nail a few two-by-fours together, and the Coca-Cola Company gave me a tin sign to attach to it. We built a little box on top of the stand, and Mother put a pot of petunias that trailed down and bloomed all summer. She didn't want the front yard to look too bad.

Then I chipped some ice from the ice box in the kitchen to cool my drinks and opened up for business. My market shifted from the woman on her front porch to insurance salesmen and other thirsty people coming down Oak Street.

Business grew, and soon I was buying cases of twenty-four Cokes for eighty cents directly off the Coke truck. That doubled my profit to forty cents per case. I expanded my line to Nu Grape and Orange Crush, and Mother convinced me to buy my own ice from the ice man instead of chipping what I could from hers. The ice man came down the street in his horse-drawn carriage selling twenty-five-pound blocks for eight cents, and if a block was broken he would give it to me free.

Soon I had earned enough money to buy my first bike. I paid Werner McElroy, who lived three doors down from us, four dollars for it. It didn't have fenders, but it had a good frame and would get me where I needed to go. I've never bought anything in my life that I appreciated more than that bike.

In winter I continued to generate my own income by selling magazine subscriptions door to door. I sold *Ladies' Home Journal* for fifteen cents a copy and made four cents profit, or the *Saturday Evening Post* for a nickel, earning a cent-and-a-half profit. You can guess which one I tried to sell first. But if they didn't buy the fifteen-cent magazine, I quickly pulled out the other, because a cent-and-a-half profit is better than nothing.

I also helped another boy with his newspaper route. He was three years older than I, and I followed his instructions carefully. Even at that young age I wanted to do my best at any job I did.

My mind wasn't totally on business, however. When I knocked on the door of a house up the street, I met Jeannette

McNeil, and my heart skipped a beat. She was beautiful; I learned later that her mother made costumes for stage performers and Jeannette had been singing on stage since she was three years old. She had real charisma. And I, with my speech impediment, was terribly shy. I immediately had a crush on her that I have never gotten over. I was a year ahead of her in school, and never said anything to her about my feelings, and later we moved out of the neighborhood. I didn't see her again for ten years.

When I turned twelve, I was old enough for my own paper route, and I carried *The Atlanta Journal* on my bicycle to homes around our West End neighborhood.

I began to contribute indirectly to the family at that point. As I mentioned, most of the grocers allowed their customers to keep charge accounts. But sometimes Mother would ask me to buy a few things, and instead of charging them to my parents' account, I would pay for them myself. I saw every week that my father still contributed nothing financially, and Mother needed my help. The little bit I offered, however, could not keep the debt from growing.

CHAPTER THREE

Building a Paper Route One Customer at a Time

I was fourteen years old in November 1935 when President Franklin D. Roosevelt came to Atlanta to dedicate Techwood Homes, the nation's first federally subsidized housing project. A short while later our family moved into one of those new units, 466 Techwood Drive, Apartment 22.

At the age of fifty-six, Mother was tired. Running a boarding house for over a decade had worn her out. Plus our family was, for all intents and purposes, bankrupt. We owed thirty-five dollars at the grocery store, and there was no way we were going to have that much money anytime soon. Moving out of the neighborhood while owing so much money disturbed Mother terribly. She believed that somehow, someday she would pay the money back, but she didn't know when or how. It wasn't until I was in the military service that I accumulated enough to repay. When I showed up with the money so many years later,

Above: Truett, second from right, and his brother Ben, far left, were annual winners in contests to sign up customers for The Atlanta Journal *newspaper.*

23

the grocer had forgotten about it. But Mother and I hadn't.

When we moved to Techwood Homes in 1935, my older siblings had grown and moved out, so only my younger brother, Ben, and I were at home. The family determined that with my father's meager income from selling insurance policies, along with money Ben and I could earn from newspaper routes, we could cut our expenses and pay the rent and utilities, sixty-seven dollars a month.

Ben and I were given responsibility for the entire Techwood Homes project, nine city blocks of multi-story apartments, for *The Atlanta Journal*, an afternoon newspaper. We both had delivered papers in West End, but Techwood gave us a different kind of challenge. Every apartment was new, so every subscriber was new. We didn't inherit a base someone else had created; we built our own business one customer at a time. We had plenty of competition from *The Atlanta Constitution* in the morning and *The Atlanta Georgian*, another afternoon paper. And, of course, many people took no newspaper at all. I had to prove to each customer that I would do the job right, then follow through on my commitment.

The key to succeeding with a paper route—and the restaurant business, I would later learn—is to take care of the customer. I had to do the job whether I felt like it or not. If I was

---

I asked several Chick-fil-A Operators to explain how the principles we believe affect the day-to-day operation of their restaurants. Their comments, like Shane Todd's at right, appear on special pages throughout the book.

"We just love our team."
Shane Todd, Athens, Georgia

When people ask what we do differently, I tell them, "Don't come visit us looking for any gimmicks or gadgets." We just love our team. We smile at them and tell them we love them. We share their joys and stand by them through their hard times. It's amazing how that filters down to our customers.

For example, I'll be here tomorrow morning at 6:30 with two dozen Krispy Kreme doughnuts. For them to see me here with my shirt and tie at 6:30 when I could be in bed goes a long way toward showing my appreciation for them.

Once a quarter I rent a van and take our college-age employees to tour the home office in Atlanta. They all meet Dan Cathy and as many other executives as we can. I did that even when I was in Raleigh, North Carolina The only difference was I had to rent hotel rooms for folks.

But more than what I do for them, it's what they do for our customers that makes a difference. Bennie McKinnley works the register for us in the morning, and recently she saw a picture of one of our regular customers in the newspaper. Bennie took it upon herself to cut out the picture, have it laminated, and surprise him with it on Monday morning.

Of course, those kinds of opportunities are few. What most customers appreciate are our smiles. We don't tolerate a bad attitude.

Melissa Beard is our Drive-Thru Queen. I get more individual compliments on her than anything else we do. She's so patient with customers who can't hear well or moms who have kids screaming out their orders. She walks them through the order deliberately and gets it right, offering suggestions, and always tells customers it's her pleasure to serve them. By the time customers get to the window, they've already had an awesome experience.

running a fever, or if we were in the middle of a thunderstorm, or electrical lines were on the ground, or we had an ice storm, my customers expected their papers to be delivered.

To keep my customers—and it's always easier to keep a customer than to replace one—I did more than sling the paper haphazardly toward the front door. I put it where the customer asked me to put it.

Elderly customers often had a rocking chair beside the front door, and I placed the paper in the chair seat so they wouldn't have to bend over. Some people had dogs running around and required me to put the paper behind the screen door. It might have been easier to tell the customer, "You put the dog, up and you won't get a chewed-up paper."

But you don't do that—not if you want to keep that customer. The customer is always right, and I always oblige the customer.

Jimmy Collins, long-time president of Chick-fil-A, talks about how I built my restaurant business in the beginning the same way, with customers that other restaurants ran off. The people who came to my first restaurant had been eating somewhere other than with me, so I built my business on those cast-offs.

Ever since I was a teenager delivering newspapers, I have tried not to lose a single customer. I treated each one like the most important person in the world, and delivered each paper as if I were delivering it to the front door of the Governor's Mansion. That's an image that still works to improve customer service. If you were working in a restaurant and suddenly the President of the United States showed up, your voice and facial expressions would change. You'd be eager to serve the President well, make sure he had a clean table, then go up and see if everything was all right, or if he needed anything. If we're willing to do that for the President, why not treat every customer that well?

My friend Mike Mescon, dean emeritus of Georgia State University's College of Business Administration, tells the story of ordering a Coca-Cola with no ice at a restaurant (not Chick-fil-A). The girl behind the counter brought a Coke with ice.

"I ordered it without ice," Mike said politely.

So the girl put her fingers over the top of the cup, poured the Coke into another cup, filled it to the top, and handed it to Mike.

Maintaining his composure, he asked, "Could I have another Coke with no ice and no fingers?"

I don't know if he ever went back to that restaurant.

Atlanta's Varsity drive-in restaurant was the first to show me the importance of treating the customer right. It was only a mile away from us when we lived in Techwood Homes, and it was *the* hang-out place for teenagers. I did most of my courting at The Varsity. Frank Gordy, the owner, was always there to make sure customers were taken care of correctly.

Our favorite curb servers were Flossie Mae, who dressed in an outrageous hat that looked like a giant fruit basket, and Hot Papa. Despite earning only a nickel or dime tip from teenagers and college students, they always gave us good service.

Courtesy is cheap to provide, and it pays great dividends. My satisfied newspaper customers sixty-five years ago became my cheerleaders, and they boosted my business. When a reader of *The Georgian* complained that his paper came late, or not at all, my customers responded that theirs always arrived on time. Pretty soon I had another customer whom I hadn't directly solicited. The most effective way of promoting my business didn't cost me anything but a little kindness.

My success as a newspaper delivery boy also depended upon my capabilities as a business manager. I bought my papers wholesale and sold them retail, and it was up to me to decide how to make a profit. Most customers paid weekly—twenty-five cents. A few paid two weeks at a time, and I always had a few who didn't want to pay at all. Whenever I knocked on the door, no one answered. So I'd watch, and if I saw a light on inside at 10 P.M., I'd try to collect then and keep them from falling more than a couple of weeks behind. Others would lag behind on purpose, then move away without paying. I lost that income, as well as the wholesale cost of the papers. Some people will beat you out of money if they can.

Techwood Homes turned out to be a great place for a paper route. I earned pocket knives and T-shirts and other prizes from the Journal for attracting new customers. I also won a trip to Jacksonville Beach—awarded to the paper boys with the most new customers—every year. They loaded us into the back of a newspaper truck and carried us down there, where I saw the ocean for the first time. My family never left town except to visit relatives occasionally, so those beach trips were my vacation.

I delivered papers at Techwood Homes until I joined the army. It was more comfortable in winter than most neighborhoods because I made deliveries out of the weather. I also got my exercise running up and down the steps. On summer evenings people brought chairs outside and visited, giving us a strong sense of community, and Mr. Drinkart, superintendent of the project, maintained the place with respect. I didn't dare cut a corner and step on the grass, or he would call my hand on it.

Sometimes at night I would walk out and lie down in that well-manicured grass, gaze up into the sky, and realize the presence of the Lord, despite our dire financial circumstances.

On Saturdays during football season, Georgia Tech played its games at Grant Field, just a couple of blocks away from our apartment. For a while I had a job selling peanuts in the stands. Later I bought my first car (a Hupmobile that cost me ten dollars; it didn't have a battery, so I always made a point of parking on a hill to get an easy rolling jump-start), and I drove people from distant parking areas to the stadium for a tip.

Sunday morning was a critical day for a newspaper delivery boy. I had to start long before daylight to take care of all of my customers. The Sunday paper was too thick to fold and too heavy to carry more than a few at a time. The fathers of some paper boys would help their sons deliver Sunday papers, especially in bad weather, carrying the bundles on the running board of the car to designated drop points every few blocks. My father never did. I often felt cheated—especially on Sunday mornings during my early teen years—because I did not have a loving and caring father.

My Sunday school teacher recognized somehow that I had a father who never told me that he loved me. Or perhaps he saw in my demeanor that I was a boy who had never said "I love you" to my father. I think he sensed my isolation, because he reached out to me and became the model of a loving and caring father.

My teacher's name was Theo Abby. He owned a small company that supplied steam fittings, and he and his wife had two sons. One of them, Ted, was my age. Through his teaching Mr. Abby gave me a better understanding of the Bible, but more important, he displayed to me a loving and caring spirit. He visited Techwood Homes often to see me and others in our Sunday school class. He also invited us occasionally to go with him and Ted to his cabin on Lake Jackson. There I witnessed a loving relationship between a father and his son.

In time I came to understand that I could choose the type of model I would follow in life, and I chose the example of Theo Abby. Now when I encounter children whose fathers do not participate in their lives, I try to establish a relationship with them. I have taught thirteen-year-old boys in Sunday school for nearly half a century, and through that contact I have tried to identify those boys who didn't have fathers or who lived in divided homes. I often give those children more attention than I do those with a stable home life. Over the years I have become a substitute father or grandfather to dozens of children, as Mr. Abby did for me sixty-five years ago.

FINANCIAL PROBLEMS FOLLOWED MY FAMILY to Techwood Homes. Even at sixty-seven dollars a month, we could not afford to live in the government-subsidized housing without the income Mother had generated running the boarding house. My father's profits from selling insurance remained close to zero, and Ben and I didn't make enough money with our newspaper routes. My sister Esther, who never allowed her childhood bout with polio to stop her, had taken a teaching position and sent ten or twenty dollars a month to help us. But even that wasn't enough, so we located a house on Myrtle Street, just off Ponce de Leon Avenue east of downtown Atlanta, and Mother came out of retirement and went back to work cooking for boarders.

I maintained my paper route back at Techwood Homes even after we moved away, and my business grew on my understanding that customers are always looking for somebody who is dependable and polite and will take care of them. It's ironic that in those years on the few occasions when I went into a department store, I was treated royally, even though I had little money to spend. The salespeople dressed well, wearing clothes similar to the merchandise they were selling, and were well mannered and groomed. Nowadays the high-fashion stores have difficulty attracting and training good people, and their customer service is becoming a lost art.

My success with the paper route convinced me that I would one day open a business of my own, most likely a service station, grocery store, or restaurant. As a high school student, I had a choice of attending college preparatory schools, Tech High or Boys' High, or I could attend Commercial High in downtown Atlanta, which offered courses geared for boys who did not plan to go to college. I chose Commercial High, where I took business courses such as bookkeeping and typing. To graduate, I also had to pass shorthand, which never interested me. When I flunked the course, I realized I would have to switch my "major" from business to bookkeeping and stay in school for another year and a half to graduate. Then my kind principal reviewed my transcript and told me that I could switch to Tech High and graduate on time without repeating shorthand. I jumped at the opportunity.

Before I left Commercial High, however, I took an elective course called Everyday Living (EDL), which turned out to be one of my most meaningful high school classes. Our EDL teacher taught us about common courtesies as well as common sense—how to dress for an interview, to remove your hat in an elevator when a lady is present, how to present yourself to a stranger.

He also introduced us to a book by Napoleon Hill that had just been published, *Think and Grow Rich*. In it Mr. Hill wrote, "Whatever the mind of man can conceive and believe, it can achieve."

I wasn't all that bright—I had difficulty keeping up in class—and I had always carried with me a bit of an inferiority complex regarding socializing at school. I was already losing my hair and never felt confident about dating girls. But I enjoyed my work, and I enjoyed the rewards of working. As I read Mr. Hill's book, I realized I could do anything if I wanted it badly enough. His words motivated me and showed me that I live in a do-it-your-self world.

The Bible says, "All things work together for good to them that love the Lord, to them who are called according to His purpose" (Romans 8:28). I never thought that would mean my balding head would keep me out of World War II, but it did. Instead of being sent to the front lines, I fought the war with a typewriter.

When I graduated from high school, I went to work as an administrative clerk for an army major at the Atlanta Ordnance Depot (now known as Fort Gillem). I skipped three pay grades to replace a man who was thirty-five years old, in part, I believe, because my thinning hair made me look older than I was.

My position put me in contact with the upper echelons on the post, and I was able to avoid the draft for awhile. When I was eventually drafted, the commanding officer and his adjutant requested that I be assigned to a position in Atlanta. In other words, no boot camp for me. I still needed six weeks of basic training under army regulations, so they assigned an old retired sergeant working on the post to train me. We would march up and down the street in cadence—just the two of us—quite conspicuously, with him barking orders, and people would go by laughing. They thought I was being punished.

That time in Atlanta turned out to be a gift from God, for if I had been sent overseas I would have missed some wonderful final days with my mother. My parents had finally retired from the boarding house business and moved to Jenkinsburg, Georgia. My sister Esther had bought a home there and invited them to live with her. It was not fancy living; the house had no indoor plumbing. But those were sweet days. My father started going back to church again and was much more pleasant to live with. On Fridays I would hitchhike down to spend the weekend with them, and Mother still wanted to take care of me. On cold nights she would heat an iron by the fire and put it at the foot of my bed to keep me warm. I and various family members installed a bathroom and running water in the house to make it more livable; Mother finally could relax.

I eventually had to leave Atlanta when the company commanding officer sent me to administrative school in Illinois for two months. I was promoted to corporal and assigned to military personnel under the chief petty officer. The greatest impression he made on me was a negative one. I waited to speak to him one day, and was sitting where I could see him and he could see me, but he never recognized me, as was his prerogative as a superior officer. My military duties were easy, but the experience was like a prison sentence because of situations like that.

Near the end of the war I finally came out from behind the desk and was assigned to a medical unit in Fort Lewis, Washington, for overseas duty. While waiting to ship out, however, I developed a strange sensitivity to sunlight. The slightest exposure to skin that was not normally exposed made me break out in hives. If I rolled up my sleeves out in the sun, the rash would appear in a matter of seconds. It rained almost every day at Fort

Lewis, but the limited sunshine we got seemed to make my problem worse.

I went to the infirmary and was put in the hospital, where doctors would give me medication and send me out in the sun. Nothing they gave me seemed to work. There was no way they could ship me out to the south Pacific, as was the army's intention. They might have sent me back to a desk job, but instead the doctors recommended that I be discharged. I was out!

I got on a train bound for Georgia by way of southern California, and at every stop along the way if the sun was shining, I forced myself out into it—first for just a few seconds, then for longer periods until my strange sensitivity disappeared.

My discharge turned out to be a special blessing. Shortly after I arrived back in Georgia, Mother, who was sixty-five years old, had appendicitis that was misdiagnosed as indigestion. By the time the doctor realized what was happening, her appendix had ruptured and peritonitis had set in. I was thankful to have had those last few visits with her.

CHAPTER FOUR

Priorities and Total Commitment

A reporter once asked me how I would like to be remembered. I answered, "I think I'd like to be remembered as one who kept my priorities in the right order. We live in a changing world, but we need to be reminded that the important things have not changed, and the important things will not change if we keep our priorities in proper order."

When World War II ended, my brother Ben and I decided we wanted to go into the restaurant business. Ben had all of the restaurant experience between us—a short time working at The Varsity near the Georgia Tech campus.

A friend of mine in College Park, Price Morton, operated the Dutch Kitchen, a twenty-four-hour restaurant, and through him we learned of an opportunity with a new restaurant company called Little House. In the years following the war, several restaurant companies had opened hundreds of small diners across the country. Among the most successful was Toddle

Above: The original Dwarf Grill, located on North Central Avenue in Hapeville, Georgia, opened its doors for business in May 1946.

House, out of Memphis, which had 151 restaurants in 1946 and was growing quickly. Toddle House built tiny, ten-stool restaurants that could be operated by a grill man, a waitress, and a dishwasher. The menu offered little more than breakfast items, hamburgers, and dessert, and customers knew they could get in and out in about twenty minutes, any time of the day or night, seven days a week.

Other companies followed the Toddle House model in designing their twenty-four-hour restaurants, including the owner of the Dutch Kitchen, who was creating the Little House restaurant chain. Ben and I each wanted a Little House franchise, and we understood from the owner that we would get them following a training period. So for seven weeks we worked twelve hours a day, seven days a week in training. At the end of our training, the owner of Little House restaurants told Ben and me that we could share a restaurant, but we would not each have one. We felt that was less than what had been promised, so we decided to strike out on our own.

Neither Ben nor I had much money, but we were determined. I sold my recently purchased Chevrolet, and we pooled our resources to come up with $4,000. Then we borrowed $6,600 from the First National Bank of Atlanta, and we were naive enough to think that for $10,600 we could buy any part of the world we wanted. We found a lot in Hapeville, 461 North Central Avenue—right on Highway 41, the main north-south thoroughfare connecting Florida to Michigan. The property was across from the brand new Ford Motor Company assembly plant and near the Atlanta Airport, good sources of potential customers. The lot measured 50 feet wide by 150 feet deep and was sandwiched between two houses. One of the homeowners, Mrs. Ruby Hammond, owned the vacant lot and hoped our restaurant would succeed so that we would later buy her house as well. The other next-door neighbor also hoped for a future opportunity to sell to us. (We eventually bought both houses.)

We bought the lot from Mrs. Hammond for $2,500 and were preparing to build our restaurant when we learned that we had to get the property rezoned for business. This was a new concept to us. Ben and I knew nothing about zoning. So we went down to Hapeville City Hall and made our application. The neighbors didn't oppose us, and the city approved our request for a zoning variance. After that brief delay we were ready to build.

We hired a carpenter to design, engineer, and build the whole thing. Our seven weeks in the short-order restaurant business proved valuable at that point; we had seen what worked and what didn't in a small restaurant. With our input, the builder drew the plan on one sheet of paper, then went to work for us on a cost-plus-10-percent basis. Ben and I did much of the manual labor, digging footings for foundations and the like. We worked as fast as we could, generating no income until we opened the doors.

We soon ran into another roadblock—a shortage of building materials. The war effort had consumed virtually every scrap of steel and copper in America, and lumber was almost as scarce. Large contractors bought almost everything that was available, so I had to beat the bushes for material. For $100 I had bought an Army surplus Jeep, which I drove from McDonough to Jackson to Jenkinsburg, calling on every hardware store around and buying all the nails they would let me have—usually five pounds at a time. Knowing the framing would later be covered with walls, Ben and I bought used lumber, and we continued working side-by-side with our carpenter.

As we were finishing the building, we began to look all over town for used equipment. We bought a stainless steel refrigerator from the Majestic restaurant on Ponce de Leon Avenue and displayed it proudly. We bought our first grill for thirty-five dollars. Then we found ten stools and four tables with chairs, and printed a limited menu offering breakfast items, a small steak, a hamburger, and a few other items, but no chicken, because it took too long to cook.

On May 23, 1946, Ben and I opened the Dwarf Grill (later renamed the Dwarf House), with first-day sales of $58.20. Our work was just beginning!

Ben was married and had a child, which meant family obligations that I had not yet undertaken. He was a go-getter, a winner who worked hard, but more of the responsibility for keeping the restaurant open fell to me. I rented a room in the house next door from Mrs. Hammond for forty-five dollars a month so I could make myself available at any hour. If the cook or the waitress needed me after midnight, they walked across the parking lot and tapped on the window. Occasionally a dishwasher or a grill man walked off the job in the middle of a shift, and I would have to get out of bed, put on my clothes, and run the grill the rest of the night, cooking eggs and flipping hamburgers. The parking lot was gravel, so if I heard a lot of cars crunching over it in the night, I got out of bed to see what I could do. In those early days, it seemed, I grabbed a few hours of rest whenever I could and spent the rest of my time in the restaurant.

Starting the restaurant and pouring all of my worldly possessions plus everything Ben and I could borrow into it taught me the full meaning of the word *commitment*. Everything was at stake. I was totally committed to the task of building a

"I'm at the restaurant most of the time."
Constantine Zouboukos, Birmingham, Alabama

I spend a lot of time at my restaurant. I think that's the biggest difference between the more successful and less successful restaurants. Some Operators are exceptional business people— much more organized than I am with charts and other tools that allow the restaurant to run smoothly even when they're not there. I prefer to be at the restaurant myself, and I think my team prefers that too. I don't mean every hour of the day, but I'm there most of the time.

Discipline is another factor in our success. My parents were strict, and I attended a military academy for high school, so I was exposed to rigorous discipline. Along with that came proper manners: "Yes sir, no sir, yes ma'am, no ma'am." I'm a stickler with rules. Following rules and procedures allows us to get every order right every time, and it means customers can always count on consistent quality.

Understanding and following procedures also allows us to be most productive during our busiest times. Everybody stays busy and focused on the job at hand, and that helps hold down stress levels and keep morale high.

At least one person a day tells me we have the best drive-thru around. I make a point of putting our best people at the headsets. I don't work the headset myself because I don't have the best voice in the restaurant. You have to have the best at that position.

And I do all the hiring myself. We have only two young women on the team right now that I didn't hire. I was out of town when they came in, and they were so exceptional we had to have them right away.

successful business, and I knew I could not fail.

We were not so committed to financial success, however, that we were willing to abandon our principles and priorities. One of the most visible examples of this was our decision to close on Sunday. Ben and I had attended Sunday school and church all our lives, and we were not about to stop just because we owned a restaurant. Our decision to close on Sunday was our way of honoring God and directing our attention to things more important than our business. If it took seven days a week to make a living with a restaurant, then we needed to be in some other line of work. Through the years I have never wavered from that position.

FOLLOWING THE EXAMPLE OF MY SUNDAY SCHOOL TEACHER from my teenage years, I offered my services at church as a teacher. When you consider the issues we face with teenagers today, you might think the boys I began teaching in Sunday school half a century ago had it easy. The 1950s, after all, were a much simpler time. But all children need strong adult role models, and many of them, even back then, weren't seeing them at home. I enjoyed treating the boys to dinner at the Dwarf House one night during the week. It was a good time for us to get to know each other between Sundays.

I was teaching eleven-year-old boys in those days (I got promoted a few years later), and I challenged them to read the entire Bible before they finished my class. I promised them a reward if they did.

One of the boys who took me up on the challenge was Harry Brown, a kind of scared little boy who was new to town and slow to make new friends. I learned that Harry's father was a traveling salesman who was out of town a lot.

The year I taught Harry was tumultuous for him. His father came home from a business trip one night and learned that Mrs. Brown had sold the piano to buy a refrigerator. (They had been without a refrigerator for several months.) In a rage, the father stormed out of the house and didn't return. Mrs. Brown, who had three boys under fifteen years old, had never worked outside the home and had no marketable skills. She went to cosmetology school so she could get a job to support her family.

Harry and several other boys worked hard throughout the year to read the Bible. Each week I asked them how much they had read the week before, and we charted their progress. At the end of the year I was proud to present Harry with his own personal Bible for having completed his reading.

We moved out of the neighborhood and joined a different church, so I lost contact with Harry Brown. But I prayed that the seeds we sowed would take root and grow.

Years later, when we opened the Chick-fil-A restaurant at Southlake Mall in Atlanta, a man came over to me and introduced himself. It was Harry Brown. He was surprised when I remembered him and the Bible he had earned so many years earlier.

We hadn't talked long before I realized that Harry, who worked for Southern Bell, was still reading his Bible and still growing in its message. He and his wife, Brenda, after taking foster children into their home for three years, were house parents at Christian City Home for Children in Union City, Georgia.

They invited me over to meet their children, and I visited them often, usually with sacks full of Chick-fil-A Chicken Sandwiches. Sometimes I would bring a troubled boy from Sunday school. Harry would tell him about his own experiences with a father who had abandoned him.

Harry and Brenda loved working with the children. One day while I was visiting with them Harry told me, "The longer I live and work with the children, the less I enjoy working at Southern Bell."

I did not know then the ramifications of that statement.

Ben and I had to be patient in the early days as we built our business. We didn't have any money for advertising. We had to build our restaurant on satisfied customers, one at a time. We were profitable from the very beginning—we had to be. But the profit was skinny, and we kept our overhead low to maintain it.

These days people come up with a concept for a restaurant chain, borrow as much money as they can, rent a fancy office, and start out with the image of success. Sometimes these high-powered business people find themselves overextended. I like our concept better. We stayed on top of our expenses and never faced a bill we couldn't pay. We earned our reputation and good name, relying on Proverbs 22:1, "A good name is better to be chosen than great riches, and loving favor rather than silver and gold." People trusted us to pay our debts on time. They learned that I could handle any problem but a financial problem.

The key to our success, I am convinced, was our commitment. When we're fully committed to something, we're not likely to give up or become discouraged, and we're not likely to fail. Commitment works in our business life as well as in our relationships with our families and with the Lord. When we're fully committed, strange and unusual things happen.

Had I not been fully committed to the success of the Dwarf

House, any of a number of roadblocks might have put us out of business: food shortages, a difficult labor market, the need for more customers.

Our greatest challenge initially was a limited supply of meat following World War II. We worked with several suppliers, but none of them could fill our needs. They were rationed in the amount they could buy, and they wanted to fill the needs of their larger, more established customers first. We needed help.

I came to know Mr. Whitton, who lived in Hapeville and was manager of the Kimble House restaurant at Five Points in Atlanta. I mentioned our problem to him, and he offered to buy a couple of extra boxes of bacon and sell them to us. Then I learned of a slaughterhouse nearby in Jonesboro that bought cows directly from farmers and had the beef inspected before selling. I negotiated with them to buy sides of beef. We ground our own meat and cut our own steaks, and maintained a reputation for good meat and quality food. At the same time, Ben and I began to understand why nobody else was going into the restaurant business in those days.

In addition to meeting the challenges of finding food and supplies, the task of keeping a restaurant open twenty-four hours a day, six days a week was grueling. Ben and I were working seventy-two-hour weeks—or longer. When a grill man or a waitress didn't show up, I found myself working double shifts. Once I worked thirty-six hours at a stretch, eating meals between flipping eggs and cutting meat. Sundays became my salvation. I knew if I could just make it until Sunday, I would have a full day to recuperate.

People have asked why we didn't close at night, and the answer is simple: We needed every customer we could get. It was discouraging, though, to step outside our empty restaurant at two in the morning and stand in the middle of Highway 41 with no cars in sight in any direction. (Nowadays we do more business at the original Dwarf House at 3 A.M. than at 3 P.M. because of airport and Ford plant employees working different shifts.)

Our reward came in the morning, when our loyal customers gathered for breakfast and coffee. The Dwarf House was just a couple of blocks from city hall, so city leaders and others would meet at our restaurant every morning. Some people have said that more real estate deals closed at the Dwarf House than at City Hall. I worked hard to memorize the likes and peculiarities of our regulars. Many of them would eat the same thing every day, maybe a sandwich with mustard and no mayonnaise, or eggs cooked a certain way. One customer always wanted one egg sunny side up and one over light. I began preparing his order when I saw him in the parking lot.

I learned that some customers are extra hard to please, so I worked harder to be their friends. I was coming back from the bank one day when a customer stormed out the side door. Something had obviously upset him terribly.

"Is everything all right?" I asked.

"I'll never eat with you again," he huffed. "I've been one of your best customers, but I'll never come back!"

"What's the problem?" I asked, trying to settle him down.

"Well, I came in here before another guy, and I was sitting at the counter, and he got his hamburger before I got mine."

I offered him a free meal, but once somebody makes a statement like that, it's weeks before he'll come back. But eventually he did, and we didn't speak of the incident again.

"We have the spirit of a servant."
Charles Gibson, Baybrook Mall

The first time I visited a Chick-fil-A restaurant, the people behind the counter smiled at me so much as I walked up, I wondered if they knew me from somewhere. Then I tasted the sandwich, and I knew I could sell that product to anybody.

That's the feeling I've tried to deliver for as long as I've had a Chick-fil-A franchise. We care about people and want to offer them a great product. When customers come here they fall in love with the spirit of Chick-fil-A.

Two things set our people apart: We're happy to be here, and we have the spirit of a servant. In our restaurant, both of those feelings must come from me, the Operator. I have to be on fire every day, and the fire must be genuine. I could give a motivational speech every day, but most people wouldn't remember what I said. But if the feeling is in my spirit, it's there every day for my team and our customers to see.

Customers pay attention to smiles. I've had them say to me, "There's not a time that I've come in here when I haven't seen a smile on your face." That's good!

I began my career as an accountant and never anticipated that I would experience this kind of good feeling for more than a decade. I've never worked as hard as I have at my Chick-fil-A, and I've never enjoyed work as much.

I've learned that you don't worry about how much or how hard you work if you enjoy it. That's the wisdom I hope to instill in everybody who works at my Chick-fil-A restaurant. I tell every student, "Find something you enjoy, and you will succeed. There's no way you can not succeed because you'll get up every day trying to do your best and enjoying it."

Our closest competitor in the early days was Pete Arnette's Bus Station. Pete was a friend of mine; I ate with him sometimes. He sold a trademark hamburger that was smaller than the bun, and he had a running joke with some customers.

"Pete, there's no meat in this bun," a customer would say. "I took a bite and got no meat."

"Take another bite," Pete would reply.

"I still don't taste any meat."

"You bit over it!"

Dave Garrett, longtime CEO of Delta Air Lines, said he knew only two places to eat in Atlanta, the Dwarf House and Pete's place. Delta employees knew if they wanted to get to the chief, they should come to the Dwarf House at lunchtime.

We built our business and made friends at the same time, always seeking to meet their needs wherever we could. If we learned that a customer was in the hospital, we sent food to the house. Likewise, if a customer died, we sent food to the family. We still do that, and customers respond with their loyalty. We're now feeding third and fourth generations of customers at the Dwarf House. Three customers have been so loyal through the years, we gave them a 1946 menu that they can order from anytime: coffee for a nickel, breakfast for thirty-five cents, a waffle for a quarter, a steak for sixty-five cents.

One of the first people to come to work for us at the Dwarf House was Jesse Reed, a Black teenager who washed dishes, scrubbed floors, and performed numerous other jobs. When Jesse started college in about 1948, he suggested that I hire his cousin Eddie White as his replacement. I interviewed Eddie and immediately liked him, and I appreciated his commitment to excellence. No matter the job, cutting potatoes or cleaning the grease trap—a reservoir that collects grease and keeps it out of the public waste water system—he always did his best work.

Although Eddie was only twelve years old, he was as big as many sixteen-year-old boys. The government didn't have regulations against hiring preteens to work part-time, and that was a good thing for Eddie's family. Eddie was the oldest of seven children. His father sometimes worked two jobs, and his mother stayed home with the children, taking in laundry to generate additional income. The White family needed whatever income Eddie could generate.

I came to learn that they were a close-knit family. Every morning Mrs. White lit a fire in the wood stove and cooked breakfast for her family of nine to enjoy together. In the evening they gathered around the table again for supper and a time for sharing the day's experiences.

When Eddie turned sixteen, he could not afford to buy a car, so on weekends several of our employees—James Martin, Bill Adams, or my sister Gladys—or I would often let him use ours. He was the kind of responsible teenager that we all could trust with our keys and know he would be careful.

As he approached his senior year in high school, I asked Eddie what he wanted to do when he finished. He said he hoped to become a medical missionary someday. He wasn't concerned about wealth. He just wanted to help people. But financial pressures at home led him to consider dropping out of South Fulton High School, working at the Dwarf House full time, and earning his high school diploma at night.

"I won't have any part of it," I told him.

I went to his home and spoke with his father about the importance of an education. We worked out a plan whereby Eddie would work after school and on weekends—forty hours a week—then contribute half of his income to the family and keep the other half.

Eddie waited a year after graduating from high school to enroll at Morris Brown College. During the interim I taught him how to be a butcher and how to cook. The waitresses took a mayonnaise jar and made a label, "Eddie's College Fund." Whenever a customer would compliment the food, they would say, "The young man who prepared it wants to go to college." People contributed quarters, dollars, and more, and when it came time to register, Eddie counted it. He didn't have all he needed, and I was proud to write a check to make up the difference.

Eddie graduated with a pre-medicine degree but did not have enough money for medical school. He came back to work for us for a year while he earned a teacher's certificate, then made a successful career in education, eventually becoming an assistant superintendent.

More than fifty years after we became friends, Eddie and I have remained closely in touch, relishing each other's successes, and sticking by each other during difficult times.

The pattern that developed with Eddie continues today. The restaurant business gives us a wonderful opportunity to mentor young people and help guide them toward adulthood. Hundreds of thousands of teenagers have worked at a Chick-fil-A restaurant, and I like to think we have been a positive influence for each of them.

Chick-fil-A franchisees (we call them Operators) take special care in selecting and working with teenagers who work in their restaurants, modeling for them positive character traits. Many of our young employees have been encouraged by their parents to work for Chick-fil-A because of the positive influence of our Operators.

"I stated and showed clearly what I expected."
Margaret Wilson Phillips, Commerce, Georgia

When it came time to train at my new restaurant, rather than send the team to other restaurants, I did a two-hour training shift in the morning and another one at night. That allowed me to state and show clearly my expectations—exactly what I wanted the customer to experience—and it worked like a charm. We talked more about philosophy than technical issues. After you understand the philosophy of Chick-fil-A, the rest comes easy.

Yesterday a man came to me representing a major food chain in the West and asked, "How do you attract the caliber of people you have in your restaurant? What's your secret?"

"If I could bottle it," I said, "we'd all be rich."

I can only speak to my experience. I was attracted to Chick-fil-A by Truett Cathy's attitude of caring, and I stay because of that. I hope I can attract the same kind of people because of the caring attitude I carry in my heart.

I've seen hundreds of instances where people will leave a purse or a wallet with credit cards and cash, and they're always returned intact.

What I love to see is the new employee carrying a tray for a woman with children. I haven't taught that, but I reinforce it with praise.

I hope through my example that I can raise the bar for young people working with Chick-fil-A. Their parents have done their job, preparing them to step out into the world. I want to give them a positive role model—an example that can make a difference in their lives as they continue to mature. That's a wonderful opportunity.

In 1973 we established the Team Member Scholarship program to encourage restaurant employees to further their education. In 1996, we replaced the Team Member Scholarship with the Leadership Scholarship program, which places a greater emphasis on an employee's community service and leadership abilities. To be eligible for the $1,000 scholarship, restaurant employees must complete their high school education, enroll in college, participate in their schools and communities, demonstrate a solid work ethic, and possess strong leadership abilities, good teamwork, and a desire to succeed.

In 1997 we awarded the first S. Truett Cathy Scholar Awards, which provide additional $1,000 scholarships to the top twenty-five Chick-fil-A Leadership Scholarship recipients each year.

According to the Council for Aid to Education, no other company in terms of size gives as much in the scholarship area as Chick-fil-A, Inc. At the beginning of the new century more than 16,000 students had taken advantage of this opportunity. A statue stands in downtown Atlanta to commemorate these scholarship students and the institutions they have attended. The twenty-three-foot-tall, twenty-foot-wide arch sculpture depicts on a grand scale people lending hands to help other people climb an archway constructed of books. An inscription at the base reads, "No goal is too high if we climb with care and confidence."

SOON AFTER WE OPENED, THE DWARF HOUSE became a headquarters for school kids. A young boy who was in my Royal Ambassadors group at the Baptist church came to work at the original Dwarf House, and one afternoon I found him smoking a cigarette in the kitchen. I was greatly disturbed to see this young person developing a terrible habit, so I said, "I have a home-work assignment for you. I want you to take two sheets of pa-per and write a list of the advantages of smoking on one sheet and disadvantages on the other. Then bring your lists back to me tomorrow."

I expected him to come back with a long list of disadvan-tages, such as cancer and needless expense, and no advantages. Instead he had three things listed as advantages. First, he got to take a smoke break. Second, smoking kept him from doing some-thing even more detrimental. Third, he was buying cigarettes from my machine, so I was making a profit.

Well, his third point really set me to thinking. After all, I made more profit out of that square foot of space the cigarette machine was sitting in than any other square foot in the restau-rant. I didn't have to do anything. The cigarette company brought in the machine, serviced it, and gave me a portion of the profit.

At the same time it had led this teenage boy, and perhaps others, to take up a deadly habit. It was a difficult decision, but I finally had the guts to get rid of it. I called the cigarette com-pany and asked them remove the machine.

THROUGH THE YEARS, MANY COURTSHIPS—some that led to mar-riages—have started over a Coke and a sandwich at the Dwarf House. People still tell me I served them their first hamburger off the grill. Some afternoons I would be the only one with just one straw in my Coke. A customer in the restaurant told me one day, "Truett if you don't get out and do some courting, you won't ever get married."

Well, I wasn't even thinking about getting married. I be-lieved I had more important things to do. About that time, however, I was reintroduced to my childhood sweetheart, Jeannette McNeil. Looking back on our courtship, it's a wonder she married me. Most of our "dates" were spent sipping a Coca-Cola at the Dwarf House and dropping nickels into the juke-box. I got off work at 10 P.M. on Saturdays, and sometimes I would take her to a late movie. After awhile she would shake me to wake up and tell me the movie was over, and it was time to take her home. I was exhausted most of the time. Sunday evening was about the only time we had together.

I loved Jeannette, and I believed she loved me, so I made plans to take a Saturday afternoon off and drive with her up to Chattanooga on the pretense of visiting my sister Myrtle. My true intention was to take Jeannette up to Lookout Mountain, where we could enjoy the spectacular view and the quiet forest, and I would propose marriage.

We walked through the woods for awhile and I looked for just the right spot. Finally I stopped, looked at her, and asked her to marry me. She affirmed her love for me, but did not say yes. Not yet. On Sunday evening, though, alone at the Dwarf House sipping Cokes, she accepted my proposal.

Hoping and believing her answer would be yes, I had earlier bought a 60-foot by 125-foot lot on Sylvan Road in East Point to build a home. My brother Horace, who did construction work in his off hours, and I built a two-bedroom, one-bath house in time for the wedding on September 19, 1948. The house was nothing fancy, but I was proud to carry Jeannette over the threshold in my arms. It was a wonderful new beginning for us.

JEANNETTE MADE AN IMMEDIATE IMPACT on my spiritual life, for while I had been a committed Christian, her level of commitment showed me a new way to live. She hadn't had a father in her home growing up, so she had to rely on the Heavenly Father, committing her life to the Lord when she was five years old. Her mother did not attend church, but that didn't keep Jeannette from getting involved, especially with her singing talent.

She also began tithing when she was in elementary school. I had not been a regular tither prior to our marriage, and Jeannette led me to begin tithing systematically. We have enjoyed the blessings of that decision throughout our lives. When we focus on what we can contribute, I learned, joy abounds.

Sir John Templeton, the financial investment expert and creator of the Templeton Funds, tells audiences that the safest recommendation and the one that pays the greatest dividend is tithing—giving 10 percent of your earnings to honor God in the way you see fit. I had an opportunity several years ago to meet him and ask for myself. He confirmed the statement and added that he had never known anyone who had tithed for ten years who was not rewarded.

My riches are my family and my foster children. I try to store any material wealth in my hands, not my heart, so that I always feel free to give it away when the opportunity arises. And I pray for discernment to know when and how to give. After a magazine article in California misquoted me by saying that I was "looking for ways to give away money," the requests came so fast we didn't have time to open all the envelopes. Many of the letters began with, "The Lord told me . . . ." One man wrote that he needed a red car with a white top, and listed the extras he desired. Another wrote: "The Lord told me not to borrow any more money, but to write you. The Lord said, 'Mr. Cathy is going to pay off your indebtedness.'" His request was for $250,000.

Jeannette also led me into a deeper prayer life. Without the ability to pray together, I doubt we could have made it. Prayer changes things. So does encouragement, and Jeannette has given me an abundance of it. When I speak to groups I like to ask them, "How do you know when somebody needs encouragement?"

After a moment of silent pondering, I answer, "If they're breathing!"

Everybody needs encouragement, and Jeannette has encouraged me every day of our marriage.

Because I usually worked the Saturday evening shift, my brother Ben sometimes would take the afternoon off and go flying. He and Horace both had pilot's licenses. On a Saturday afternoon in 1949, Horace and Ben planned to fly to Chattanooga for an air show. Ben finished his shift and completed the report sheet at two o'clock, then drove to the airport. They and two other men rented an airplane and took off, even though weather reports predicted storms moving in.

When the sky turned menacing, they landed in Rome and waited. The storm passed, and an hour after sundown they took off again, even though my brothers were licensed to fly only in daylight and the plane they had rented did not have equipment for flying at night.

They never made it to Chattanooga. A man on the ground near Dalton saw the plane flying low and signaling SOS with blinking wing lights. The man called the state patrol, who quickly organized a makeshift lighted runway of car headlights shining on a wide field.

My brothers saw the lights and attempted to land, but a

wing tip hit a patrol car's radio antenna. Whichever man was piloting the plane gunned the engine to take it back up, and it rose about thirty feet, but then fell flat like a pancake and burst into flames. Ben and Horace, my only brothers, were both dead.

The loss hit me particularly hard on Monday morning, when I saw where Ben made out the report sheet on Saturday afternoon in good health. I realized again that he would never be back, and my tears flowed. A year later I bought my brother's share of the business from his wife, Eunice, and for several years afterward I saw that she and their daughter, Nancy, were provided for.

In the meantime, Jeannette spent many hours in the restaurant doing whatever had to be done to take care of customers—waiting tables, running the cash register, whatever was needed. She continued in that role long after our children were born.

BUSINESS AT THE DWARF HOUSE CONTINUED TO GROW, and I began looking for a place to build a second restaurant. I found the ideal location on a corner in Forest Park, across from the entrance to the Atlanta Ordnance Depot, where I had served part of my time in the army.

If I could open a restaurant there, I could give folks a good skillet egg and fresh fried bacon, instead of those eggs we got in the army that tasted like they had been refrigerated for a year.

I began to research who owned the property, but because I didn't have a backlog of funds, I wasn't rushing the deal. I learned that a man named Yancey owned it, along with a nearby service station. I approached him about selling the corner lot.

"I've owned that land for years," Mr. Yancey said, "and it's just been sitting there doing nothing. But I sold it to a man two weeks ago."

Disappointed and curious, I asked, "Would you mind telling me what you sold it for?

"Three thousand dollars."

I was surprised that corner lot sold for so little.

"I wish I'd known about it," I said. "I could have handled $3,000."

The more I thought about the missed opportunity, the more disturbed I became. I began to pray about it, asking God's guidance. With His nudging, I decided to find the purchaser and offer to buy the property from him at a profit. So I drove back to the service station to ask Mr. Yancey who he had sold the property to. It was early in the evening, and before I reached the service station I pulled the car to the curbside and prayed for guidance and direction about what I should do.

As soon as I drove into the station, Mr. Yancey came to me and said, "You were the one interested in that piece of property on the corner, weren't you?"

"That's right," I said.

"Well, the fellow who was going to buy it said he had some unexpected expenses and asked if he could renege on the purchase. If you're still interested, you can have it for the same price I sold it to the other fellow."

I had to hold back tears. If I had given up and not followed God's urging to go back to see Mr. Yancey, I would have missed my opportunity again.

As we prepared to construct our second Dwarf House, I began to understand why the property might have been priced so cheap. The lot had no city or county water lines to it, and the well was contaminated. Neither was there public sewerage. We cleared those hurdles, however. The city extended the water line to us, and we installed a septic tank, which had to be pumped every week. I seemed to be undergoing an endurance test, but we built a customer base.

OUR CHILDREN, DAN, DON ("BUBBA"), AND TRUDY WERE BORN between 1953 and 1955, so when I left home for the restaurant every morning, Jeannette had her hands full. As they grew, she would pile them all into the Mercury—the boys sometimes fighting like cats and dogs—and bring them to the Dwarf House.

When they got out of the car they all knew they couldn't come inside without picking up a discarded can, bottle, or paper sack in the parking lot and putting it in the trash can. They later took on additional responsibilities, such as scraping gum off the bottom of seats and tables with a screwdriver or razor, or restocking the candy display by the cash register.

The waitresses, grill men, and manager became to them Aunt Zelma, Aunt Annie, Uncle Henry, Uncle Paul, and so forth. The waitresses enjoyed playing with the children, and sometimes would dress one of them up in a white apron— pulling it all the way up to the armpits so it wouldn't drag on the floor. They would then walk over to a table with a pad and pencil, ask the customers for their orders, then pretend to write it down. (The waitress would stand close enough to overhear the order.) Sometimes the customers would leave the children a nickel or dime tip. The kids figured out how that worked real quick. Other times Jeannette dressed the children up as dwarfs and they sang the "Dwarf House Jingle" to customers.

We were all family, working together. For us, family, business, and church weren't separate aspects of our life. They all blended in together. Those early experiences shaped our children's viewpoints about life and work.

Business often remained on my front burner even when we were traveling on family trips. In the early days we never took an entire week off—I couldn't turn the restaurants over to someone else for that long. But we would take off on a Saturday afternoon, head down Highway 41 for Florida, and return on Monday night.

We made lots of stops along the way, and not just for bathroom breaks. Whenever I saw a fast-food restaurant I hadn't visited, I stopped, went in, and observed their operations, taking away ideas on what was or wasn't working. All the time the kids just wanted to get to Florida so they could jump into the Atlantic Ocean. In fact, they always had a contest for who could see the ocean first.

On one trip to Daytona Beach we were one block away from the ocean, and I wanted to stop at a Steak 'n' Shake that looked particularly fresh and clean. "Aw, Dad!" came the chorus from the backseat. "We're just a block away."

"I'll just be a minute," I insisted, but they were not convinced.

I was true to my word, however, and came out quickly.

"Thanks, Dad, for not staying so long," but their words did not drip with sincerity.

While we were in Daytona, they took more opportunities to say, "Thanks, Dad, for not staying so long at the Steak 'n' Shake," as if I would have spent our entire vacation checking out restaurants. The line became a running joke in our family, and even today one of the children will say, "Dad, we want to thank you again for not staying so long at the Steak 'n' Shake."

CHAPTER FIVE

Out to the Farm

Jeannette and I were city folks. We both grew up in Atlanta, and we had no plans to move out to the country. With three children, however, we were quickly outgrowing our two-bedroom, one-bathroom house on Sylvan Road. We could almost shake hands with our neighbors through the bedroom window. So we bought a vacant lot in Hapeville where we planned to build a larger home.

But it wasn't just the house and lot that cramped us. It was city living in general. The restaurants demanded at least twelve hours of my time every day—time spent with crowds of people coming in and out. Of course, I loved that aspect of my life, but when I went home, I needed peace and quiet, and I wasn't getting that in the city.

We also came to realize that we didn't want our children to grow up in the city. That fact became evident when a neighbor boy from two doors up the street came to our house one day and invited Dan over to fight.

Above: The Cathy children in 1959: from left, Bubba, Trudy, and Dan.

In 1956 we met Frank Harbin, who said he wanted to sell his farm out in Clayton County for $29,000 so he could buy a lot in the city and build a house on it. We went out and looked at the farm—262 acres that backed up to the Flint River—and decided that perhaps the country was the place for us.

My dad, who had moved back into the city and came to the Dwarf House often, thought I was out of my mind for going into debt and paying that much for a piece of property. He had gone broke with real estate during the Depression, and he believed we were due for another downturn every twenty years. But we bought it anyway.

The farm had a two-bedroom, one-bathroom house on it, so we didn't buy ourselves any extra indoor living space. But ours was the only house in sight at the time. It was set in a pine thicket on a rise that looked down across a wide pasture toward the river. In the barn were a tractor and all the attachments, and out in the pasture stood one lonely cow. Mr. Harbin had raised cattle on his farm, and had rounded up all of them when he left. But he never could catch that one cow, who remained with us for several years.

Someone told us shortly after we bought the property that we would be living in the midst of a bunch of bootleggers out in the country south of Atlanta, and that didn't give us a good feeling. But we soon learned that bootleggers make good neighbors—they keep to themselves.

Growing up on the farm was a great experience for our children. They enjoyed the outdoors and were exposed firsthand to many of God's creations. I remember walking through the fields with them singing the song Jeannette had taught them, "God's beautiful world, God's beautiful world, I love God's beautiful world. He made it for you. He made it for me. I love God's beautiful world."

Jeannette did so much for our children spiritually. Her education at New Orleans Seminary prepared her to lead them in Bible study. She also provided an incredibly nurturing, warm, accepting home, while setting high expectations for our children to do their best, to be their best, and to not forget who they were or Whose they were. All this despite the fact that Jeannette's father left the family when she was six months old, and she never experienced a strong positive family background as a child.

Trudy, our youngest, was a sponge when it came to her mother's teaching. When she was six years old she told Jeannette she was ready to accept Christ. Neither of her older brothers had made that commitment, and when Jeannette told Dan what was up, he and Bubba rode their bikes down the road to a grove of walnut trees and had a talk. They were ready, too, but it had taken their little sister's public declaration to push them. The next Sunday night they all went forward, and a week later they were baptized together.

Jeannette has always put the children and our business first in her life. She has never taken time for a gardening club, bridge club, or other ladies' activities. She has made herself available to the rest of us and any unexpected opportunities that might arise along the way.

These days I surprise her by bringing home foster children unexpectedly. When I get a call that a child needs our help right away, I have to respond. I try to call home before I show up at the door with an extra mouth to feed, and Jeannette is always ready for us.

When we moved to the farm, I learned that the stars shine brighter out in the country, and the world is a lot quieter there.

I found it to be just what I needed after working with the public all day in the confines of a restaurant. I could go out and put up a fence, Bush-Hog some brambles, or feed the cows and horses we acquired over time. In our forty-plus years there we have added on three times, but we're still in the original house.

As the children grew we bought trail bikes for them to enjoy, and they rode all over the farm. I enjoyed riding with them. Later Dan and Bubba saved their money and bought a motorcycle. I've loved motorcycles since 1937 when I bought an Indian Scout from Ted Edwards, whose dealership was behind The Varsity restaurant facing Spring Street in Atlanta. (I think I pushed that Scout more than I rode it.)

I rode the boys' Kawasaki so much, my family decided to buy one for me for my birthday. I returned from a business trip and found it parked in the kitchen. I climbed on and started it up right there, and as the kitchen filled up with smoke, Jeannette ran in saying, "Get that thing out of the house!"

I haven't stopped riding my red Electra Glide Classic 1990 Harley-Davidson, although Jeannette doesn't ride with me. She says she stays near the phone when I'm riding.

Several years ago some men from First Baptist Church in Jonesboro, including our pastor, Dr. Charles Q. Carter, organized regular motorcycle trips. We call ourselves the Holy Rollers, and we ride all over the Southeast. One weekend we rode up to Charles' first pastorate in Kentucky. We have also made several trips to Daytona Beach.

When we stop along the way, people often say to me, "You don't look like a Harley rider." Then I start to roll up my sleeve, and I say, "Let me show you my tattoo." (Of course, I stop before I roll it up all the way and reveal my unadorned arm.)

Dan has organized a similar but much larger group of bikers at his church. They'll have forty or fifty bikers attend church, then afterward ride down to Callaway Gardens for lunch. During Bike Week they all rode down to Daytona Beach.

Like life on the farm, motorcycle riding allows us to enjoy the beauty of God's creation up close, and I am thankful for the opportunity.

CHAPTER SIX

Next Time I'll Go All the Way

One of the boys in the Sunday school class I teach came out to the farm for dinner and brought his nine-year-old brother with him. After the meal I asked, "Would you like to walk into the woods and look for wild animals?"

"Yeah! Yeah!" they both hollered.

So we took the path behind the house and walked into the woods down toward the river. The sky began to grow dark as evening came upon us, and I grabbed a stick and threw it into the woods without their seeing me. We all stopped when we heard the sound, and I said, "I think I hear one of those wild animals."

The nine-year-old grabbed my hand, and we walked more slowly and much more quietly. They didn't say anything else, and I began to realize that Stevie truly was frightened by the woods and the darkness. He didn't want to go all the way to the river. We stopped, and I knelt down beside him.

Above: The rebuilt Dwarf House in Forest Park was one of Atlanta's first fast-food restaurants.

"Stevie," I said, "you don't have to worry about anything. God is with us. He'll protect us."

"I know," Stevie said, " but I'm scared of the dark. I can't sleep at home without the light on. I'm afraid of the night."

"Would you like to go back now?" I asked.

"Yes," he said.

So Stevie, his brother, and I turned and walked back out of the woods. We emerged at the edge of a field, and we walked out to the highest peak on the property, where the sky had lit up with the moon and stars.

"Why don't we sit here and meditate and pray together for a few minutes," I suggested.

Stevie offered a prayer apologizing to the Lord for being scared. "I know You're with me, Lord," he said. "You're going to protect us. Next time I'll go all the way."

Then he hesitated and added, "I might not go *all* the way, but I'll go part of the way."

I smiled there in the dark. Stevie was being completely honest in his prayer.

When I pray I try to pray as honestly as Stevie did that night, from the heart, not just with words, but with thoughts, seeking God's guidance and direction, committing myself to do what I should do and to change what I should change.

We need to trust the Lord in our various circumstances. We all need God in our lives. But sometimes we're not willing to go all the way with Him. Our faith is not complete. When we do offer our faith completely, we experience complete peace and joy, knowing that God is watching over us regardless of our circumstances.

A SERIES OF EVENTS IN 1960 led me to my own crisis of faith, and like Stevie in the woods, I wasn't ready to go all the way. I was afraid of the dark.

For nearly ten years I had operated two Dwarf House restaurants and had long since given up the idea of further expansion. Both restaurants were successful, and I probably could have continued building a new restaurant every five years as I had planned. But it didn't take long to realize that two was plenty. It was like having two full-time jobs. If I wasn't having problems in one, I was having problems in the other, and I asked myself, "Who needs more problems?" On a cold night in February my "problems" were reduced by half.

When the telephone rings after midnight, it rarely brings good news. In the early hours of February 24, 1960, the news was that the Forest Park Dwarf House was on fire. The temperature was six degrees that night, and when I got to the restaurant firemen were doing all they could in the icy heat. But before the sun rose we all knew it was a total loss.

I carried only $25,000 worth of insurance on the building, far too little to replace it, so to reopen would mean a trip to the bank for a mortgage.

Then came more bad news. I passed some blood, and Jeannette insisted that I see a doctor about it. Tests indicated that I had polyps that would have to be removed from my colon, and the doctor said I would need about thirty days to recover before returning to work. The timing couldn't have been worse; I had a restaurant to rebuild and another one to operate. But after a time of prayer with Jeannette, I found peace in my situation and decided to look at it as a month-long vacation— something I had never done.

The operation and my recovery turned out to be anything

but a vacation. I had a horrible allergic reaction to codeine, and I awoke from surgery in terrible pain. They pumped my stomach to remove what was left of the drug, but the reaction continued. They kept me in the hospital for two weeks before sending me home totally exhausted. It was several more weeks before I could think productively about what to do about rebuilding in Forest Park.

Not too many months before my surgery I had bought a coffee maker. Now, you might not think such a decision would have a long-lasting impact, but this one did.

I have always looked for better ways to do things, and when I learned about a truly automated coffee machine, I had to see it in operation. The company that supplied our equipment, Whitlock Dobbs Inc., arranged a demonstration.

Commercial coffee makers in those days resembled the home brewing equipment that we use today. You put in a filter and coffee, and the machine sprayed water through. Then you took the bag out of the top, dumped out the grounds, and started over again. Every pot tasted a little different because everybody put in a slightly different amount of coffee.

But with this new coffee maker, I could put coffee in a bin, hook the machine up to the water supply, and it did the rest. All I had to do was push buttons, and it measured the coffee and water, made the coffee, dumped the grounds, and washed itself. I bought the first one in the Atlanta area, and our customers became the first in town to enjoy the most consistent cup of coffee around.

Consistency, I had learned, is important in the restaurant business. Customers don't like surprises. If they have a good experience, they want to repeat that experience—all the way down to the coffee.

During the process of buying the new coffee maker, I met Jimmy Collins, the young kitchen designer for Whitlock Dobbs. When I later talked with his company about designing the equipment for our new restaurant in Forest Park, Jimmy took on the assignment.

The fire had completely cleaned the slate, and I knew I could do whatever I wanted with the new restaurant. Atlanta was not leading the way in restaurant innovation at that time, so I traveled around the country looking at various operations to see what might work best for us. McDonald's was just getting off the ground nationally, along with several other fast-food restaurant chains. I was fascinated with the self-serve concept. It reduced labor, streamlined operations, and sped up service. The systems could also deliver consistency, which I knew would bring customers again and again. I wrestled, then, with whether to stick with the coffee shop operation that had worked so well for us, or go for the latest self-service design.

That same year, 1960, Jimmy Collins and I, along with our wives, went to the National Restaurant Association meeting in Chicago. There Jimmy and I spent most of our time talking about the possibilities for the Dwarf House in Forest Park. I decided to go with a fast-food restaurant, with no table service. We would be one of the first restaurants in the Atlanta area in this emerging aspect of the restaurant business. Jimmy took my ideas for the kitchen in the new restaurant and gave me the design I wanted.

THEN CAME ANOTHER SETBACK. Six months after the polyps had been removed from my colon, additional polyps appeared. Never before or since have I been more demoralized.

The first operation, which was supposed to have been so simple, had almost killed me. Now the doctor said he would have to remove a section of my colon to ensure the polyps would not reappear. I was thirty-eight years old, and I did not expect to come home alive. Jeannette was more hopeful. "Truett," she said, "God isn't finished with your life yet. I don't think He's going to take you."

I didn't share her optimism. I would have given my last dime just to keep from having to return to the operating table. Jeannette drove me to the hospital the next morning, leaving our three small children at home.

In those moments I came to realize that the material things I had acquired, the success I had enjoyed with the Dwarf House, meant nothing. What mattered was my relationships with Jeannette, Dan, Bubba, Trudy, my friends, and most of all, my relationship with God. I experienced a new peace in the car that morning, knowing that whether I lived or died I would be with God.

I awoke in the recovery room surprised to see Jeannette's face. I had survived. And I was not in pain. The second operation and my recovery were a picnic compared with the first. I remained in the hospital for several days, and whenever I could I visited the hospital chapel and sat at the foot of a cross mounted on an altar.

"I'm alive," I prayed again and again. "Thank you, God, that I'm alive."

Although I don't believe I had squandered money on material things up to that point, the experience reminded me first-hand what was important and not important. I learned the true value of life and was changed by that understanding. Certain things happen in life that strengthen our faith and remind us of our need to put our lives in the hands of the Lord. I came out of the hospital a new creation, prepared to take on whatever life dealt, for I knew God would be with me.

WE OPENED THE NEW DWARF HOUSE in a beautiful octagonal building with lots of glass and a new style of doing business—fast-food counter service. A national restaurant magazine put us on the cover and wrote about how we were the forerunner in our field.

I realized by the end of our first day of business, however, that I had made a terrible mistake. Customer after customer sought me out to tell me, "We don't like this. We like for a waitress to come and take our order. We want our coffee in china cup with a waitress there to offer a refill."

They didn't like the new concept of standing at a counter to give their orders and waiting for their food to be delivered. Many customers absolutely refused to clean their tables when they left, leading to additional problems. A doctor who ate with us often came to me and said, "Truett, I'll clean up my mess when I leave, but I won't clean up behind somebody else."

I quickly became discouraged. I had borrowed $90,000 from the bank, the most money I had ever borrowed, and gone through the agony of designing and building a new restaurant so people would come eat with me. But the customers I had served for so many years didn't want anything to do with my new restaurant.

My entry into the fast-food business left me sleepless at night. I had spent fifteen years building my business in the two restaurants, and I would likely lose both of them if the new concept didn't work.

I called my good friend Ted Davis, who owned Davis Brothers Cafeterias, and asked him for advice. Ted came out and watched the operation, and he liked what we were doing. He advised me to stick with it, knowing that I would replace the old customers I lost with even more new customers. But I didn't want to lose *any* customers.

I learned something about myself in those days: It was terribly unrewarding for me just to ring the cash register in a restaurant and collect money. I'm motivated in my business by the compliments I receive for our service and food quality.

A few weeks later I called Ted Davis again. He had been thinking about opening the first Kentucky Fried Chicken restaurant in Georgia, and he said, "If you'd like, I'll lease your building and buy your equipment."

To consider giving up a business where I had spent most of the previous ten years of my life was heart wrenching. Yet I was so beaten and worn out, his offer to take the operation off my hands was a godsend. I took his offer, and the lease helped me pay off the loan and gave me additional income.

God has a better plan for us than we have for ourselves. When I was suddenly relieved of the responsibility of a second restaurant, I had time to ask, "What's next for Truett Cathy?"

It was time for me to pray the words of little Stevie, "I know You're with me, Lord. You're going to protect us. Next time I'll go all the way."

It was about that time that I met a man who truly knew the meaning of going "all the way," and I learned a lesson from him.

Forty years ago the whole world knew of Paul Anderson,

"The World's Strongest Man." A native of Toccoa, Georgia, Paul had won the gold medal for weightlifting at the 1956 Olympic Games in Melbourne, Australia. Back home the next year he lifted an incredible 6,270 pounds in a back lift, the greatest weight ever raised by a human being. Setting world records at an event in Russia as a member of the first team of its kind to go behind the Iron Curtain, he became known as "*chudo piryody*," a wonder of nature. All of Georgia was proud to call Paul Anderson our native son.

One day in 1961 a white Econoline van emblazoned with huge red letters, PAUL ANDERSON, WORLD'S STRONGEST MAN, rolled through town with Paul Anderson himself riding behind on a bicycle. When I saw this great champion, I couldn't miss the opportunity to meet him personally.

Paul and his wife, Glenda, explained that they were on a pilgrimage all the way to Father Flanagan's Boys Town in Omaha, Nebraska. Paul had experienced a call from God to build a home for troubled youth in Vidalia, Georgia (home of the world-famous onions), and they hoped to generate publicity and interest along the way. I invited them to come eat with us at the Dwarf House so I could learn more.

Over a hamburger Paul and Glenda explained that their home would be for homeless and troubled young men sixteen to twenty-one years of age, the majority of whom were under court orders and would otherwise be in juvenile or adult penal institutions. Paul said his foremost purpose was to teach each young man that he was a creation of Almighty God with a special purpose in life. Once a boy gains self-confidence and positive values, Paul said, "He will reach out rather than strike out."

It was my privilege to write a check that day for the Paul Anderson Youth Home—the first donation Paul and Glenda

received. Years later, when the Andersons' home was successfully serving young men, Paul gave me the privilege of serving
on the home's board of trustees, a position I still proudly hold.

Through his commitment and his determination to go all
the way with God's help, Paul had great success with his boys.
With his size, strength, and booming voice, when he spoke,
you jumped. Paul played tough man to boys who had been in
serious trouble. They knew not to argue with The World's Strongest Man. If they didn't like his way of discipline, or if they ran
away, their only other choice was back to jail. For many boys he
and Glenda were miracle workers. They changed lives with their
encouragement.

Paul passed away in 1994, but with Glenda still at the helm,
the Paul Anderson Youth Home continues to fulfill his dream:
to strengthen America by building men of faith, men of discipline, and men of character.

He was, and continues to be, an inspiration to me.

CHAPTER SEVEN

Creating Chick-fil-A

With only one restaurant to manage, I felt like I had time on my hands. I began to look over our menu items and see what we might add or improve. We had tried fried chicken in the past but had taken it off the menu because it took too long to cook. Plus, fried chicken can be deceptive. It looks thoroughly cooked on the outside, and the juices may run clear when you prick it. But if a customer gets down to the bone and finds it bloody, that chicken will come right back at you.

Then in 1961 Jim and Hall Goode, owners of Goode Brothers Poultry, came to me in a quandary. They had been asked by an airline to provide a boneless, skinless chicken breast that would fit the plastic trays they used to serve meals on planes. The Goodes met the request, but their process left boneless breast pieces that didn't meet the airline's size requirements. They were trying to develop a market for these excess pieces. One day they brought me a bunch of them

---

Above: Truett and Jeannette (center) and Truett's secretary, Brooksie Kirk (right), introduce the new chicken steak sandwich at a convention of restaurant owners and managers.

and asked if I could do anything with them.

I knew immediately that they had provided the answer to the chicken problem. After the bone was removed, the chicken would cook more quickly, evenly, and thoroughly. Attempting to speed the process even further, I remembered my mother's method of covering the pan with a heavy top, creating something of a pressure cooker. I tried that and found that the chicken indeed cooked faster, and remained more moist as well. Then I discovered the recently introduced Henny Penny cooker, a pressure cooker that used oil and could cook a boneless chicken breast in four minutes, start to finish. Cooking so quickly meant we wouldn't have to cook our products ahead and hold them in a warming cabinet or under a heating lamp. All our chicken could be served fresh.

Still looking for the best way to serve the chicken, I put it on a buttered bun instead of on a plate all by itself. But it still wasn't exactly right. The meat needed seasoning and a nice breading. The development process was only beginning. I worked for years, adding this, taking away that. I was up to more than twenty seasonings and breading ingredients—twice as many as Colonel Sanders had in his secret recipe. I knew that when I finally found the right recipe, it needed to be complicated so no one could replicate it easily.

Remembering how my mother had prepared chicken years earlier at the boarding house, I tried seasoning the meat overnight before cooking. Each time I changed the formula, I tested it on customers. I had fun in the kitchen and enjoyed the feedback. I surprised customers when I added two dill pickles, but they said it added just the right touch.

Finally, after about four years of experimentation and testing, customers said, "We like it. Don't change it again."

I folded up the recipe and put it in my pocket. I called it a chicken steak sandwich, and my customers loved it. But nobody else knew about it. I had to get the word out into the community—beyond our regular customers. I decided to buy a full-page ad in each of the Forest Park newspapers, which competed fiercely for news and subscribers. In fact, that competition spilled over into the personal lives of the publishers, Tony Grey and Jack Troy, who barely spoke to each other. Because of their high-profile positions, their long-standing feud was widely known.

I thought it would be fun, and a good thing, to get them to agree on something—anything—publicly. And what better issue to agree on than the great taste of our chicken steak sandwich? I called each man separately and asked him to come to the restaurant with a photographer. Neither publisher knew the other was coming, but when they saw each other they knew something was up.

I told them I would buy a full-page ad in each of their papers if they would sit in our circle booth side by side eating our chicken sandwich.

"Then let your photographers take a picture of you two shaking hands," I said.

I had already written the caption for the picture: "We disagree on many things, but this is one thing we agree on—this is the best chicken sandwich that we've *ever* eaten."

It worked. The ad with the photo hit the papers, and everybody in town was talking about it—wondering how I got Jack and Tony to agree on anything. Later we even got national exposure when Dr. Robert Schuller invited me to tell the story on his Sunday morning television show. He also later included the story in his book *The Be (Happy) Attitudes*, under "Blessed are the peacemakers."

Soon our new sandwich was outselling hamburgers at the Dwarf House, and I wondered how to widen our customer base even further. I gave no thought to opening another restaurant. My experience with the second Dwarf House had eliminated any idea of expansion. Instead I thought I could sell our new product through other restaurants—let them invest in the bricks and mortar and give me access to their menus.

To make it work I would need several things:
- a clever trade name for the product;
- restaurant owners who would sell the product;
- customers who would buy the product.

My business was about to undergo a huge transition. I met with a trademark attorney about registering and protecting the product name, which I had not yet conceived. He explained that I couldn't trademark "Chicken Steak Sandwich" or any other simple names. I would have to misspell a word, turn it sideways or upside down, or do something else to distinguish it.

I began to reflect on the product, which was the best part of the chicken—a boneless breast. It occurred to me that the best cut of beef is a fillet; why not call ours a chicken fillet? Or chick fillet? Or Chick-fil-A? The name literally just came to me, with the capital A—for top quality—on the end. We registered the name in 1963 and had the logo designed. That logo has been updated a few times but looks very similar to the original one produced four decades ago.

The next step was finding restaurants to sell Chick-fil-A sandwiches. I knew the best place to meet hundreds of restaurant owners at one time would be at the 1964 Southeastern Restaurant Trade Association. I got a display and some cooking equipment, and Jeannette and my new secretary, Brooksie Kirk, joined me in cooking and serving free samples of Chick-fil-A. The folks literally ate it up, and we walked away with dozens of verbal agreements. Within four months fifty restaurants were selling Chick-fil-A.

The restaurants paid us nothing for the right to sell our product. Rather, Goode Brothers Poultry Company supplied boneless chicken breasts, then paid us a royalty based on the number of pounds sold.

I often found myself on the road in those days helping restaurants get started with Chick-fil-A. As an example, a judge opened a new restaurant down in Alma, Georgia, a crossroads town on Highway 1 halfway between Hazelhurst and Waycross. The Chick-fil-A Chicken Sandwich was a perfect menu item for a man who knew little about the business, because cooking and serving it was so simple. We set him up with a Henny Penny cooker and showed him and his staff how to prepare and serve Chick-fil-A.

The day the restaurant opened, Jeannette, the children, and I all rose long before the sun, piled into the station wagon, and drove down to Alma in time to walk up and down the street passing out "Be Our Guest" cards inviting people to the new restaurant to try out Chick-fil-A. We were passionate about our product, and we wanted the restaurant owners and their customers to know it.

We continued working hard to sell Chick-fil-A through independent restaurants, and we soon hit the radar screen with a huge splash. In 1965 the world's first domed stadium, the Astrodome, opened in Houston. We were there on opening day. The Astrodome, dubbed the Eighth Wonder of the World, became a licensed seller of Chick-fil-A, as did Atlanta Stadium a year later.

We began to realize, however, that licensing our product

might not be such a good idea, for while it was one of the easiest ways to sell, it was almost impossible to maintain consistent quality. Some restaurants, for example, would cook all their Chick-fil-A breasts in the morning for the lunch crowd, then leave them sitting around for a couple of hours.

Hours before Braves baseball games at Atlanta Stadium, they cooked chicken downstairs, then put it in a refrigerator until just before game time, then sent it upstairs to be reheated and sold as Chick-fil-A. The result, as described by Major League baseball umpire Ron Luciano, was a lousy chicken sandwich. Luciano disliked the sandwich so much he wrote about it in a book years later.

I needed to control the quality, and the only solution I could think of was to open my own restaurants—a prospect that still didn't appeal to me.

In the meantime we continued to take advantage of every public relations opportunity. I learned that Lady Bird Johnson, wife of President Lyndon B. Johnson, was making a whistle-stop tour of Georgia and was going to be served Georgia delicacies like Talmadge Ham. It seemed to me that if the First Lady was going to enjoy our state's best foods, she should have a Chick-fil-A Chicken Sandwich. I called Senator Herman Talmadge, who lived a few miles away from us in Lovejoy, and reminded him that Georgia is a poultry producing state, and suggested that Mrs. Johnson should eat some chicken while she was in Atlanta. And the best chicken around was the Chick-fil-A Chicken Sandwich.

Senator Talmadge invited me to bring over some sandwiches and have lunch with him. He took a bite and said, "Gee, this is good."

I came home and told Jeannette that Senator Talmadge was

making arrangements for us to serve Chick-fil-A to Mrs. Johnson and the twenty-five people traveling with her. It was a grand opportunity.

Then the senator called and told us that Mrs. Johnson wasn't going to be in Atlanta, but Savannah, and we wouldn't be serving twenty-five, but 250 people.

Undaunted, we made arrangements through the Georgia Power Company to gain access to a restaurant that was closed during the lunch hour. Jeannette and I got our Henny Penny cooker, 250 boneless chicken breasts, buns, and everything else we needed, and drove to Savannah in our station wagon. In the meantime, we had arranged with *The Atlanta Constitution* to have a photographer on hand to take our picture with Mrs. Johnson.

Our orders were to deliver the box lunches at 12:17 P.M. When we arrived in Savannah, Jeannette and I cooked the chicken and put together the lunches, then packed them in the back of the station wagon. Two state patrolmen escorted us to the railroad station where Mrs. Johnson was speaking. The place was crowded with hundreds of people, but we got to the proper place right on time. I looked around for our photographer, but he was nowhere in sight. He apparently had gotten lost in the crowd, and we were about to miss our photo opportunity. I looked desperately for him, then looked at Jeannette. She had the answer. She had come prepared with an Instamatic camera she had received in the mail. She pulled it out of her pocketbook, and I handed the First Lady her Chick-fil-A box lunch. The photo turned out great, although it didn't make the newspaper.

Another high-profile customer visited the Dwarf House. Colonel Harlan Sanders, creator of Kentucky Fried Chicken, was in town visiting my friend Ted Davis, who had bought the second Dwarf House and converted it to Georgia's first

Kentucky Fried Chicken restaurant. Ted brought Colonel Sanders—in his traditional white suit and string tie—by for a chicken sandwich. While he was eating, Charlie, our grill man, said, "Colonel, isn't that the best chicken you've ever eaten?"

Without batting an eye, Colonel Sanders said, "Second best."

In the early days I mixed up the seasonings and breading in the kitchen of the Dwarf House and shipped them to restaurants serving Chick-fil-A. Some of the other folks in the kitchen knew a few of the ingredients, but nobody knew everything I put in, or the proportions. As we grew, I multiplied the recipe and made bigger batches. Then when it got to the point that I was mixing with pounds instead of tablespoons, it no longer was feasible for me to do it all by hand. I arranged for Goode Brothers, our poultry supplier, to prepare and deliver the seasoning and breading.

Today we go out of our way to keep people from being able to figure out our product. One company makes our seasonings, and another makes the breading.

On a cold Saturday afternoon in February 1965, potential tragedy struck. The fryer under the hood of the Dwarf House caught fire, and flames went right up to the roof. The Hapeville Fire Department responded quickly and put out the fire before the restaurant burned to the ground. Water poured out the front door and into the parking lot, where I stood watching the smoldering mess.

One of the waitresses walked over to me and asked, "When should we apply for unemployment?"

"We're going to reopen Monday morning," I said.

She looked at me like I was crazy. Nobody else would have

dreamed we would open on Monday, given the condition the restaurant was in. But I was dead serious. We had customers who wanted to eat with us, and I couldn't stand to turn anyone away. I was not going to be put out of business by another fire.

We couldn't do anything until the building was inspected by the insurance company, but the adjuster came out quickly and wrote up his report. While I waited for him to finish, I found a telephone and started calling people who could help get us back in business.

By Sunday we had at least a hundred friends, family, and contractors bundled against the cold doing what they could to help. It was like an old-fashioned barn raising, perhaps not unlike what my parents had experienced when their house burned down in 1914. An electrician who was a friend of mine called a warehouse and got the supplies he needed to rewire the building, including new light fixtures. A plumber friend made repairs in the kitchen.

The sheet rock had collapsed under the weight of the water, so we had to shovel it out and replace it. After we did all that, we painted the whole thing.

In the dark of night, at around two o'clock Monday morning, we had everything in shape to open, although the rafters were still steaming. The fire department pledged to remain on alert.

A few hours later, we opened for business as usual.

Several customers came in and said, "I see y'all repainted over the weekend."

"That's right," I said, "we sure did."

My sister Gladys had a gift shop in Greenbriar Shopping Center, Atlanta's first enclosed shopping mall, in southwest Atlanta. Whenever I visited Greenbriar I noticed that except for the coffee shop at Woolworth's, the Magnolia Room at Rich's, and the Orange Bowl, there was no place inside to eat.

"Why don't you bring your chicken sandwich down here and sell it?" Gladys suggested.

I liked the idea and immediately contacted the shopping center manager, who told me the developer wasn't interested. He believed an enclosed mall would trap smoke and fumes from cooking, and customers would drop their paper all over the place, making a mess of the center.

I suggested that if he really wanted the place to stay clean, he could lock the doors and keep all the customers out, but that would be an extreme measure. He understood my point and drew up a lease for us.

A little hearing aid store had recently closed, so we took the empty space, which was thirteen feet wide—only 384 square feet in all. When we designed the interior space, we had to make every square foot count. We put the counter all the way across the front, with a half-height door underneath so that you had to squat down and waddle like a duck to get through. We had room for only one cash register and, from the beginning, we displayed salads and lemon pie in a refrigerated case on the counter.

The staff couldn't do a lot of moving around when they were working. To determine the basic layout we marked off a 13-by-30-foot space in our office, then cut cardboard boxes into the size of the counter, the Henny Penny cooker, and other equipment. Then we moved them around until we came up with the most efficient configuration.

We decided to do all of the cooking out front, in view of the customers. In those days almost all fast-food operations depended on out-of-sight cooking. At other chicken restaurants the customer stood at the counter, and cooking took place behind a wall. A few minutes later when the order was ready, this hairy tattooed arm came through the wall with a box of chicken. We didn't feel like that was an exciting way to do it.

We wanted more animation. We borrowed the idea of out-front cooking from steak houses and grills, believing it would catch the attention of shoppers as they walked through the mall.

I sketched what I wanted and took it to Jimmy Collins, who by now had his own design firm; then I stood with Jimmy beside his drafting table as he sharpened my ideas. He incorporated several "homey" touches from the Dwarf House, such as our red shingles. When the build-out was complete, I had invested $17,000 in preparation for our opening, and the financial advantage of locating in a mall was clear. I had spent $90,000 to build a free-standing restaurant seven years earlier. My capital would go much further in this environment.

Up to that point we hadn't done any market research, but I knew people liked our chicken sandwich—we had sold thousands of them at the Dwarf House. We filled out the menu with potato fries, cole slaw, lemon pie, Coca-Cola products, and later, fresh-squeezed lemonade.

A few customers questioned whether we were wise to step out with such a simple concept. "What's so special about taking the bone out of a piece of chicken and putting it between two pieces of bread?" they asked.

"Nothing," I said. "That's why I was able to do it. But it's going to take the right people to build the business."

Doris Williams was working in a school lunchroom earning

less money than her talent warranted, and I knew she was the right person to operate the first Chick-fil-A restaurant, which opened in November 1967. My entire family worked with her to ensure success.

When we opened, we were an immediate hit. Of course, most people had no idea what Chick-fil-A was, so our children stood at the front of the store with trays of samples for customers passing by. I had to remind them not to stand there like wooden Indians, but to hold out the tray, catch the eye of a customer, and say, "Have a sample of Chick-fil-A!"

Once people tasted our product, they came back and bought more. The Greenbriar Shopping Center developer was thrilled by our success. We had negotiated a base rent, with additional money to be paid based on our revenue. We soon were paying five or six times our base rent because of our tremendous sales.

Looking back I can see that I had been preparing for twenty-one years to open the first Chick-fil-A restaurant. Income from the Dwarf House provided financial support for the new venture. (We opened seventeen Chick-fil-A restaurants before I took a dollar out of the company.) Even more important were the lessons I had learned, which helped ensure our future success.

Other people have tried to duplicate Chick-fil-A, but nobody has gotten it quite right. A man in Atlanta created a boneless chicken breast product, opened two restaurants, and delivered his product in five-pound packages to other restaurants. But he wasn't able to build a clientele, and soon he went out of business.

I cannot explain why the fast-food giants did not catch on to the idea of a chicken sandwich—some say it was divine protection—but for many years we had the market to ourselves.

CHAPTER EIGHT

Climbing with Care and Confidence

A man presented me with a business proposal for a restaurant company. He had opened five restaurants that were doing pretty well, and he considered his moderate success to be a green light for raising capital and expanding at a rate of 500 units a year.

I wasn't interested. He might be able to raise the money he needs, but to hire and properly train the thousands of people necessary to serve customers in 500 restaurants across the country would be a monumental undertaking and eventually would lead to disaster.

In all my years in the restaurant business, I have tried never to overextend. I'm satisfied stepping from one plateau to the next, making sure we're doing every thing right before moving on. Financial experts tell me our strength would allow us to open restaurants at a much more aggressive pace than our current seventy per year. But I'd rather have seventy restaurants

---

Above: The first Chick-fil-A restaurant at Greenbriar Shopping Center, Atlanta, 1967.

operating efficiently and professionally than 500 restaurants where half are run well and the other half not.

Chick-fil-A is now one of the largest privately owned restaurant companies in the country. Many others have achieved our size by offering ownership in their companies to the public. We have resisted and will continue to resist that status.

In the early days we did not offer stock for sale because I could not predict how fast the company might grow or what dividends we might pay to anyone who might invest. Additionally, I'm afraid the directors, if we had a bad year, might tell me I'm old-fashioned and fire me. Too often Wall Street analysts are more interested in profits than they are in principles and people.

Many people who are creating and running companies couldn't care less about anything but their personal bottom lines. If the stock goes down the tubes after they've sold their options, they say that's just the risk an investor takes.

If I had a widow invest her savings in Chick-fil-A and the company didn't pay the return she expected, I would feel obligated to make up the difference to her. Even if we paid less than she could earn in a savings certificate, I would feel compelled to bail her out. Feeling that way about it, I might as well sign the bank note and be personally responsible rather than take other people's money.

For that and additional reasons, we have never offered stock options to Chick-fil-A employees. If I were to bring on a person and give him half his salary in stock options, that might pay off in great dividends and growth over the long term. Plus, it would save the company considerable current cash flow.

But the value of that stock would always be determined by the profits of the corporation, and if I cut into those profits by giving away a bunch of the company's money, employees and stockholders might resent my charity.

Or an Operator with a sack full of stock options might decide to sell out after fifteen years and retire early or do something else. Our system puts the cash in the hands of the Operators today, instead of sometime down the road with a lump sum, and encourages them to earn all they can, save all they can, and give all they can right now. Their focus is on today's customer.

THE MOST COMMON REASON COMPANIES FAIL, I believe, is their desire to grow faster than they can manage. This can be particularly true with companies that make a public offering and find themselves staring at a pile of money. All they want to do is grow. But you have to digest growth as you go.

Companies may set goals, and if all goes according to plan everything works out well. But if they have extended themselves to the limits of their finances and their talent, even a slight economic downturn can force them to lay off employees to salvage the company. You don't build a good reputation by discharging people, but rather by developing people.

Throughout the 1990s, American corporations grew at astonishing rates. But as soon as bad news appeared on the horizon, tens of thousands were dismissed. I cannot run a business that way. I never want to fire someone simply to save money. I want everyone who works at Chick-fil-A to feel secure that we will not resort to layoffs because we have overextended.

When we opened the first Chick-fil-A restaurant in 1967, I never expected a chain of 1,000 restaurants, and at that time I was not capable of running such an operation. But I grew into it one day at a time with the help of talented people around me.

Although I get a lot of credit for what we've done through

the years, these days I directly contribute very little to the success and future of the Chick-fil-A business. When you get this size, you grow through the talent of others—people I have attracted through the years who make my job look easy. I divided the tasks among other people more skilled in their areas than I am, and I *trust* them to do the job well.

When Jimmy Collins came on board, I told him, "I want you to help me open restaurants and see that they stay open." I placed the greatest emphasis on "stay open." That sank in with Jimmy, and with everyone else who has come to work with us. I want everyone at Chick-fil-A to know that we don't build and open restaurants just so we can close them if they don't work out. We must be careful about how we build them, where we put them, and who we put in there to run them.

Anybody can open a restaurant. All it takes is money. But keeping one open is what makes the difference. The Dwarf House, I believe, is good representation of the kind of commitment we make and expect. After the original Dwarf House had been in business for fifty years, we checked to see how many restaurants in Atlanta were still in business at the same location under the same management. We found none. Some were still in the same family, but didn't have the same operator. Now we've been operating the Dwarf House for more than 55 years in the same location.

Not long after the Greenbriar restaurant opened, I got a call from Morrison's, the cafeteria company. They saw potential in the Chick-fil-A concept and offered me what I thought was a fancy price to buy it. They had the resources we needed to grow, and they wanted me to put together a staff to handle operations,

"Focus on customers, cleanliness, and quality food."
Ed King, Tyler, Texas

Truett Cathy told me when I became a franchisee in 1978 to focus on three things: my customers, the cleanliness of the restaurant, and the quality of the food. "Do that," he said, "and you won't have any problems in business."

He's right. It works.

Every morning when I come in, I check the condition of the parking lot and the drive-thru area and pick up any litter. We concentrate on making sure the back of the restaurant is manicured nicely. Our drive-thru customers spend a lot of time back there, and if they see that area is clean and pleasant, they can be assured that everything inside is clean as well.

Then I walk through the dining room and the playground area to see how a customer will perceive it. If any lights are burned out or the crew missed anything while cleaning the night before, we square that away.

When customers come in, we insist on great customer service, with polite team members who make eye contact with their customers and treat them with respect.

In addition to Truett's three keys, I spend a lot of time making our presence known in the community, attending meetings and civic activities or working through my church. We also have a Unit Marketing Director who keeps us involved in activities all over town. Tyler is a relatively small town (population 78,800), and we've grown with it since 1983. We have to keep reminding people who we are, where we are, and what we can do for them.

design, and construction, and other aspects of the company. I would become an officer and stay for at least five years or until we had opened 50 restaurants.

Morrison's offered a financial guarantee for me as we went forward with Chick-fil-A, and I was tempted to take them up on it. I had great respect for them. They were a southern company known for quality, and I was gratified to know they thought that much of me personally.

Jimmy Collins had not yet come to work with me, and I talked with him about coming along with the Morrison's deal as the design and construction director. He declined. He liked being on his own and didn't want to be tied to a large corporation. He added, though, that if I held onto Chick-fil-A, he would consider working with me.

Jeannette and I discussed the Morrison's opportunity at length, and we brought the children, who were teenagers, into the conversation. We often prayed together for the business, and we gathered around the couch on our knees to ask for God's guidance at this critical juncture.

My policy has always been to share my business problems with my family. It's uplifting for me to know that our children are praying for me about a business decision I must make. I also hoped that if I shared my problems with them as children, they would share their problems with me and let me help them when they grew older.

We prayed about this mountain-size decision, whether to give up all the basic control of the future of Chick-fil-A for a guarantee of financial well-being. In the end we decided not to sell out.

Looking back, the decision was clearly the right one. You can never predict what will happen when you turn over control to someone else, no matter how well intentioned they are. A good friend sold one of his companies to a group of investors who did not run the enterprise according to his high standards. The company he sold still carried my friend's name, and he believed the poor operation was a detriment to his name and reputation. So he paid the investors who had bought his company a sum of money not to use his name. Once again I am reminded of Proverbs 22:1, "A good name is better to be chosen than great riches, and loving favor rather than silver and gold."

ABOUT THE SAME TIME, WE WERE DESIGNING our second Chick-fil-A restaurant, which was going into Oglethorpe Mall in Savannah, Georgia. This time we had 1,000 square feet of space, and Jimmy Collins brought several designs, each of which didn't work for one reason or another. I was also talking with Jimmy about the possibility of coming to work full time for Chick-fil-A. He was at a crossroads in his career, having enrolled in Bible college as he considered entering the ministry.

I needed Jimmy at that point. I knew there was only so much I could do myself, and I wasn't skilled at designing and equipping a restaurant. Jimmy had those talents. I also knew that Jimmy's values and my values went hand in hand. He thinks like me on a lot of things. Jimmy hadn't told me that he and his wife had discussed my offer and decided against it. Jimmy was afraid that I wanted him to do nothing but implement my ideas and not innovate on his own. A situation like that did not appeal to him.

He needed a sign of my confidence and willingness to turn over the design aspect of the company to him. I did not know any of that the day he came in with the drawings for the Oglethorpe Mall restaurant rolled up with a rubber band around them.

"What do you think about what you've drawn?" I asked him before he pulled off the rubber band.

"This is it," he said. "We do it like this, and we've got this thing right."

"Are you sure?" I asked.

I wanted to know that he had challenged the design himself and had not found it lacking. If he could be certain, then I trusted him.

"I'm positive," he said. "This is it."

I wanted to convey my trust to Jimmy, so before he had rolled the rubber band off the drawings, I said, "Okay. This is what we'll do. Now, are you coming to work for me?"

He hesitated briefly, then said, "Yes." He had changed his mind when he understood my trust in him.

Then we looked at the new design together, and he was right. He had taken the best of what worked at Greenbriar then created a mirror image in the Oglethorpe space, allowing us to handle much higher volume. He put two cash registers on the counter, a precursor to our multiple cash-register design that allows a customer to walk into a restaurant and quickly make contact with a smiling face. We opened the Oglethorpe Mall restaurant together in 1968, and we have followed that same basic design concept ever since.

We had a hard time getting into enclosed shopping centers in the early days. Jimmy and I traveled all over the country meeting with developers, most of whom expressed the same concerns we heard from Greenbriar Shopping Center before they let us in. They didn't want food smells, litter, and chicken bones all over the place. (We had to work extra hard educating some developers that a boneless breast of chicken didn't have a bone.)

But we sold many of them on the positive aspects of having

Chick-fil-A restaurants in their malls. Not only would we generate tremendous revenue per square foot, but we would also give shoppers more time to buy from other retailers. When customers stop shopping for an hour to go out or sit down for lunch, that puts them on the sidelines in the eyes of the retailers. But when they eat with us, they can be back shopping in twenty minutes or less. The developers began to see that picture, and softened to the idea of our coming in.

One particularly tough sell was right in our own neighborhood, Perimeter Mall, on the north side of Atlanta. The Rouse Company in Columbia, Maryland, was building the mall, and Jimmy began calling on them. We had made up our minds that we had to be in there, and they had decided we were not getting in. We were a joke to them. Every time Jimmy walked into their offices, they said, "Here comes Chicken Little again!"

Richard Rich, chairman of Rich's, the largest department store in Atlanta and an anchor tenant at Perimeter Mall, wrote a reference letter for us declaring the positive impact we had on malls. Still, Rouse didn't budge.

We kept up our campaign throughout the construction process. Every time we heard that someone from Rouse headquarters was coming to Atlanta, Jimmy or I took food to them at the job site. Then Jimmy began a postcard campaign. Every day for thirty days he sent a card to Rouse with a photo of a Chick-fil-A restaurant or product on one side, and an advantage of including us in Perimeter Mall on the other.

Finally they called and said, "Cut out the postcards! We're going to make a deal!"

On August 9, 1971, Perimeter Mall opened with Chick-fil-A serving our original boneless breast chicken sandwich.

CHAPTER NINE

The Loyalty Effect

When Jimmy Collins came to work at Chick-fil-A, he knew how the fast-food business worked. He had been designing restaurant kitchens for years and had seen the high turnover rate. Anticipating a similar experience with Chick-fil-A, he wrote a plan of action for terminating a Chick-fil-A Operator. He brought the plan to me to review and approve, but when I realized what it was, I stopped reading.

"We won't need this plan," I said handing it back to him. "We won't be making any changes."

He looked at me as if he didn't understand, so I explained that with the Chick-fil-A Operator Agreement I had established at the first restaurant in Greenbriar Shopping Center, plus my commitment to selecting only the best people as Operators, our people wouldn't leave.

We would be loyal to them, treating them as we wished to be treated, and they would reciprocate. They did. Fewer than 5

Above: Loyal team members build loyalty among Chick-fil-A customers.

percent of our Operators leave the chain in any given year. Other chains tout their "knowledge management" with their computer and communications systems; we manage knowledge by keeping people—and their knowledge—in the organization. The food tastes better with that kind of long-term Operator stability.

Many factors have added up to this kind of commitment from our Operators. From the beginning, and until only recently, I interviewed every new candidate. I knew all of the Operators by name, and most of their spouses and children. Now with more than 1,000 locations, it's hard to feel that personal contact. It's almost embarrassing that I don't recognize them all anymore. But the relationships that have grown out of our times together have given us all the feeling that the Operators are in business with me, not "the company." The more we can foster the feeling that we are a group of people working together, depending on each other, and not just bound by a franchise agreement, the more likely we are to be loyal to each other.

In my first meeting with a potential Operator, I explain that our commitment is going to be like a marriage, with no consideration given to divorce. We're much more careful about selecting Operators when we know we can't easily get rid of them. When selecting franchisees, we look for individuals who are willing to make and follow through on that kind of commitment to the Chick-fil-A business. We expect our Operators to abide by several tenets that we adhere to:

- People want to work with a person, not for a company.
- Each new Operator is committed to a single restaurant.
- Operators will hold no outside employment or other business interest.
- We choose Operators for their ability and their influence, so we want them in their restaurants.

- We expect quality interaction between Operators and team members.
- We expect quality interaction between Operators and customers, both in the restaurant and in the community.

Harvard Business School Press in 1996 published a book titled *The Loyalty Effect*, which showed the correlation between loyalty and corporate profits. The author, Frederick F. Reichheld, stated, "Businesses that concentrate on finding and keeping good customers, productive employees, and supportive investors continue to generate superior results. . . . [Loyalty] remains one of the great engines of business success."

"Loyalty leaders," Mr. Reichheld wrote, "see people as assets rather than expenses, and they expect those assets to pay returns over a period of many years. Loyalty leaders choose human assets carefully, then find ways to extend their productive lifetimes and increase their value."

Mr. Reichheld used Chick-fil-A as one of his primary examples, showing how our lifelong commitment to the success and well-being of Operators has resulted in loyal Operators who then experience tremendous loyalty from their team members—and in turn, their customers—especially when compared with the rest of the quick-service restaurant business.

We have created this "loyalty effect" at Chick-fil-A through a unique relationship with our Operators. After we make the necessary investment—buying the real estate and building the restaurant—we turn over the responsibility of running a $2 million-plus business (for a free-standing location) to these independent franchisees—many who have not yet turned thirty years old. We support them with training, technology, and anything else they need. But the bottom line depends on the Operator's honesty, integrity, commitment, and loyalty to customers and to us. We trust our Operators to make good decisions—and they do.

I don't know of another restaurant company that places so much responsibility in the hands of its franchisees. Other companies consider it too risky. In our case, though, the extra measure of trust has brought us the success we enjoy today. The Operator is the CEO, manager, president, and treasurer of his or her own business.

I haven't changed the basic agreement with Operators since my first Chick-fil-A restaurant opened in 1967. Our franchise agreement calls for the Operator to pay Chick-fil-A 15 percent of gross sales plus 50 percent of net profits from the restaurant as a service charge. When I selected Doris Williams in 1967 as the first Chick-fil-A Operator, I guaranteed that she would earn at least as much as she did from the school lunchroom, and she wound up making much more than that. We still guarantee a base return to Operators to ensure that they can meet their personal needs while opening a new restaurant or turning around a difficult situation.

Our Operators work closely with us, but they are owners of their own business. In 2002 more than half of our Operators earn more than $100,000, many earn more than $200,000, and a few top $300,000.

The first question most people ask about our agreement, and the first one Mr. Reichheld asked, is, "How could you afford such a generous arrangement with Operators?" The answer is obvious. We love it when an Operator earns a lot of money because that means we are also earning a lot of money from the restaurant. The more successful we make the Operator, the more successful we are. We want the Operator to take the same attitude: "The more successful I make Chick-fil-A, the more successful I make myself." Our Operators are in business for themselves, but not by themselves.

The second question they ask is, "Why do you close on Sunday, the biggest day of the week for many restaurants?" The answer lies in loyalty. For my family and me, when we speak of *loyalty* we first mean loyalty to God. Closing our business on Sunday, the Lord's Day, is our way of honoring God and showing our loyalty to Him. My brother Ben and I closed our first restaurant on the first Sunday after we opened in 1946, and my children have committed to closing our restaurants on Sundays long after I'm gone. I believe God honors our decision and sets before us unexpected opportunities to do greater work for Him because of our loyalty.

Another key to Operator loyalty lies in our decision to allow each Operator to have only one restaurant. At first this policy might seem counterintuitive. Many companies reward success by enlarging territories or bringing them into the company to oversee operations of other franchisees. I want our best people right there full time in the restaurant they've built, serving the customers and team members who have become loyal to them.

Jimmy Collins likes to say, "If you aren't selling chicken, you'd better be supporting somebody who is." A few Operators believe that because they have trained their staff well, their presence isn't needed. But I've found that team members will always perform better when the Operator is on site. We also realize the importance of taking care of the Operators' families. That's a secondary reason why we close on Sunday—so Operators and

"The customer in front of you is funding your paycheck."
Alex Rodriguez, Atlanta

When you reach a certain volume of sales, the temptation may be to focus on speed. I choose, however, to first make sure every order is filled correctly, even if that means moving a little slower.

The bottom line is, the customer standing right in front of you is funding your paycheck, and perhaps your future. Treat that one person right. Give him or her all of your attention for the moment. Then, when you've served that customer, you can move on to the next one.

My role as Operator is to model the kind of behavior I want my crew to practice. That makes it doubly important for me to have compassion for the customer and to have a servant's attitude. That can be hard if a customer is sounding off in the middle of lunch. But the customer is always right, even when he or she is wrong.

When my crew sees me treat a customer with respect even in a difficult situation, they're more likely to do the same when I'm away.

I also take personal interest in the people who work in our restaurant, dropping personal notes in with their paychecks, buying cake on their birthdays, attending softball games and track meets. My goal for them is first to be successful in life, and then to be a good Chick-fil-A team member.

When their time in my restaurant has ended, I want them to know that they've worked someplace that's different.

team members can count on at least one day a week devoted entirely to family, worship, and personal pursuits.

This is one of the most important principles we live by: The family must come first. We tell Operators the worst thing that can happen, other than to drop dead, is to lose your family. What does a man gain if he gains the whole world and loses his family? We can't expect a person to be a high performer if he or she has problems at home. It's a balancing act at times, working sixty hours a week and still finding time for the family.

We remind Operators that when they go home they shouldn't watch television with the family for two hours and call that "family time." You have to focus on them. Give them everything you've got.

LOYALTY BEGINS WITH TRUST. My policy has always been to select trustworthy people—then trust them!

Several years ago I loaned money to a young man to pay for college. We agreed that he would pay back $250 a month until the obligation was fulfilled. I told him I wasn't going to try to keep up with how much he paid or how much he owed. It was up to him to tell me when it was paid off. A person will live up to that kind of trust and set a high standard of honesty.

In another case, a teenage boy works for me around our home, and sometimes drives me to or from the airport, to speaking engagements, or other destinations. At the end of each week he tells me how many hours he's worked, and I pay him. We don't keep a time card—he just tells me what I owe him. Because he knows I trust him so completely on financial matters, he is more likely to trust me when I offer advice or guidance. He knows I want only what's best for him.

That kind of trust runs throughout our company. I believe any member of our Executive Committee who describes his relationship with me would begin with the word *trust*. Our senior management team of six senior vice presidents, the president, and myself, has been together for more than twenty years because we trust each other completely.

Buck McCabe, Senior Vice President, Finance, described how he responds to that trust: "Truett trusts me with so much that I feel a greater responsibility to do my job right. I think others in the company feel the same way. It might be easier for us, and we might not work as hard, if Truett didn't entrust us with so much. He has put more responsibility on our shoulders."

Jimmy Collins told me that he is a better steward of my money than his own, and I believe him. He never overspent just because the money was coming from Truett Cathy.

Success in any relationship or endeavor begins with trust. It's amazing how much you can accomplish when you trust the people around you and they trust you.

One of the commitments we make in our Corporate Purpose is "to be faithful stewards of all that God has entrusted to us." God has entrusted us with His creation. We follow His model by entrusting the assets and opportunities of Chick-fil-A to our Operators, team members, and staff, allowing them to be good stewards of these assets. Likewise, I trust my management team to run the company from the inside. Trusting them doesn't mean I never question a decision. It's good for them to realize the decision can be challenged, and that I want them to be thoughtful in their conclusions and sure of their convictions.

I hear stories about entrepreneurs who control too much and are too arbitrary with the people who work with them. Business owners can be so intimidating that people are afraid to tell them the real truth. It's difficult to disagree with a tyrant; the consequences can be severe—and lasting.

I want people who work with me to feel completely relaxed when they take a viewpoint opposite mine. I respect their opinions—I would not have hired them if I didn't—and I want them to feel my acceptance and appreciation for them when we disagree.

As an example, we spent a tremendous amount of money on a computer system, then flew in a technician from Florida every week at a high hourly rate to program it for us. I met with our people in charge of the project and questioned them regarding the expense and the value we expected in return, and the answers were difficult for me to accept. I cannot say that I ever fully agreed with the decision, but I yielded to the people in charge of that area of our company. I trusted them to do what was best.

We now are on the leading edge of information technology among restaurant companies, which is important given the decentralized nature of our organization. Because each restaurant is a separate legal and tax entity, we make hundreds of separate tax filings and the like as a service to our Operators. We use a Web-based payroll system, one of the first in the industry, that allows Operators to write checks in the restaurant.

I don't always accede to the opinion of the Executive Committee; ultimately I am responsible for the decisions made in the name of Chick-fil-A, and I can never afford to forget that. Some people have asked if I pray for the answer regarding specific business issues. The Lord gives us a mind and the ability to use it. I pray for wisdom every day, and I believe He has granted me that. I prefer to seek His counsel on issues more vital than the day-to-day operations of the company

It's upsetting to learn that someone we have contracted with has not lived up to the trust and faith we placed in him. Back in my early days with the Dwarf House, I got a call at home at about 10 o'clock on a Sunday night. Two of my employees said they wouldn't be in on Monday morning; they were opening their own restaurant half a mile up the street. We had a small crew in those days, and it was hard to cover the simultaneous loss of two people. Not to mention the personal disappointment.

Today the most disappointing news I receive is when an Operator is taking more than his share from the cash drawer. One year just before our annual business Seminar for Operators, I learned that a couple of Operators were doing just that. I believed, however, that we could work out the situations and keep them on board. They had made a mistake, and if they were willing to own up to it, I was willing to work with them.

At our annual Seminar I stood before the entire company and announced that anyone carrying guilt because he hadn't been playing the game fairly could come to me and admit it, and I would forgive them. They would not lose their franchises, although they would have to make restitution.

No one acknowledged guilt, but it was a moving moment. One Operator came to Jimmy Collins with tears in his eyes. "I can't believe anybody would steal from Truett Cathy and Chick-fil-A," the Operator said. A month later we learned that the same Operator had taken $15,000. I cannot describe the deep disappointment I felt having been betrayed by our friend.

In recent years we had to terminate the franchise agreement of another Operator who had been with us for almost twenty years and was earning nearly $200,000 a year. You would think he would want to protect that income, if not his good name and reputation. Unfortunately, though, not everyone is trustworthy. Regardless of how much money they're making, a few people think they're paying too much money to Chick-fil-A, and they're tempted to cut a corner improperly here and there and generate some additional income for themselves.

My experience has shown me that when a person is cheating on you and lying to you, over time he will become increasingly bold until he gets caught. We have sophisticated accounting and information technology departments that usually detect when somebody is shortchanging us.

Another question we often hear is, "Why don't you offer typical franchises where the franchisee makes a substantial investment?" The answer is similar to my answer regarding a public offering, and can be found in our needs. A restaurant company needs two things to succeed, capital and talent. Franchise restaurant corporations raise capital by selling the rights—usually for hundreds of thousands of dollars—to open a restaurant to people who have already succeeded in business and are looking for a good investment. Sometimes the franchise owner will work directly in the restaurant, but most of the ones I have met are looking to own several units from which they draw income. They aren't interested in actually wearing a uniform and serving customers.

Restaurant magazines are full of articles discussing franchisees blaming franchisers for their lack of success, when the problem is their own lack of time in the restaurant.

We supply the initial capital for the restaurant, so we don't have to limit our search for Operators to people with high personal net worth. The only money required from an Operator is a $5,000 refundable initial capital commitment. To fuel the kind of growth we desire, we need eager, talented, honest, dependable, people-oriented Operators who are hungry to succeed in the restaurant business and will put their heart and soul into it. We look for several specific traits when we're seeking an Operator:

- Solid character is tantamount.
- Applicants must demonstrate that they really want the opportunity with an entrepreneurial attitude.
- They should set high standards of excellence for themselves.
- Their general appearance must be neat and clean.
- Job stability demonstrates long-term commitment.
- Financial responsibility shows me they can handle the business we entrust them with.

Motivation expert Zig Ziglar has said that among the top twenty-five attributes companies look for in an executive, not one of them deals with experience. Character traits are most important. Everything else can be learned.

We receive 1,000 applicants a month from people who desire to become Chick-fil-A Operators. As I mentioned earlier, our Operators are often young; the average starting age of an Operator is thirty years old. Most of them have been Chick-fil-A team members who are eager to succeed, and we give them a lot of flexibility in the way they lead their team. We draw certain lines in the sand where principles are involved, and we expect those lines to be respected. But we don't mind if Operators push their way right up to that line. As Jimmy Collins has often said, "We'd rather restrain mustangs than kick mules."

When we have policy briefings with our Operators, we tell them, "Don't play it safe. If you're right out there at the edge of your authority, we'll ease you back when the time comes."

We don't want to scare people into thinking they can't take any risk or push the limits of their responsibility, or we'll end up with a bunch of timid Operators. We encourage people to think and to experiment under reasonable circumstances. When you have a dynamic atmosphere, you never know where great ideas will come from. They just come.

Making myself accessible to the Operators, I believe, further encourages that dynamic atmosphere. We discourage following a chain of command; I may be the most accessible person in our headquarters. I want our Operators to know that I value our relationship as much as they do. When I talk with an Operator I give my full attention. I want to know what's on his or her mind and what we can do to make the Operator more successful.

My good friend Bobby Richardson played second base for the New York Yankees from 1955 to 1966. He and his teammates earned four World Series rings, and Bobby still holds the record for the most runs batted in during a World Series.

Knowing he had played with several of the greatest players ever—Mickey Mantle, Yogi Berra, Whitey Ford, Elston Howard, Roger Maris—I asked him, "What's the most important aspect to winning, the coach or the players?"

After thinking a few moments, he said, "The players are more important, but the coach had better select good players."

It's the same way in the restaurant business. The most important job an Operator has is selecting his people.

Some companies put up a "Help Wanted" sign, and the first person who shows up gets the job. That's not the way we select our people. You don't generally find good employees wandering the streets. We go to schools, churches, youth organizations, and other places where quality people gather and tell them what we have to offer.

When we speak to young people about job and career

"The most important people are our employees."
Roger Clark, Mesquite, Texas

The most important people in this business are our employees. Some people will say customers are most important, but if we create the right atmosphere where our employees enjoy their jobs and have opportunities for growth, they will get a kick out of their work. Then that feeling will spill right over to the customer.

It takes a special kind of person to work here—someone who wants to make others happy; someone with a servant attitude; someone who wants to put smiles on the faces of others. We set our standards high, and we hire people who can meet those standards. Good people want the bar set high. It makes them feel better about themselves and what they're doing.

We remind them that they're not just working for a quick-serve chicken restaurant. They're working to create an atmosphere. We get them involved in opportunities outside the restaurant— parades and school visits, for example—so they don't think of themselves as cashiers. They're part of a winning team. That keeps them plugged in to the overall growth of the business.

Their involvement has helped take us from a $1 million restaurant to a $3 million-plus restaurant, and we're still growing strong. We have been tremendously active in the school system. We called every school in the city looking for opportunities to serve. We give teachers "Be Our Guest" cards as incentives for students. We sometimes surprise teachers by showing up with a party tray of Chick-fil-A Nuggets or a brownie tray to thank them for the work they do.

We've involved ourselves in other community activities, but the school system has been a home run for us. Giving so much to teachers and students creates a level of loyalty that leads to long-term success for us.

opportunities, we advise them, "Select a job representing a company you will be proud to work for. Then make them proud of you." It's important, then, that our Operators represent Chick-fil-A in a manner that will attract quality people, so that everyone who works with us is proud to be a part of our team.

Most of our people are, in fact, proud to work for Chick-fil-A. We have a good name in the community—so good that many team members find when they apply for a credit card or a loan that financial institutions are eager to do business with them because they work for Chick-fil-A.

I recently had a car painted, and when I went to pick it up, the car wasn't ready as promised. I asked the manager why, and he said they had completed the job, but when they found the car was for Chick-fil-A, they reevaluated the quality of their work and decided to repaint it. If you enjoy a good reputation, people treat you better.

Occasionally I'll go into one of our restaurants and see someone who obviously isn't getting the job done, and I'll ask the Operator, "Why in the world did you hire that person?"

The answer they sometimes give is, "He needed a job so badly, I hired him."

"Well, put him on the payroll," I say, "but don't ask him to show up to work. You'll be better off if he stays at home."

We don't hire people because they need a job. We hire people because we need them. We must be very selective. We train Operators to hire more than just bodies; hire people who are trainable and who will adhere to that training. We're careful even when we're hiring part-time temporary help. The wrong person working just ten hours a week can run off a lot of customers.

Hiring for and managing a restaurant is a lot like organizing a baseball team. Bobby Richardson has four World Series rings because the New York Yankees identified talent and trained them to become superstars. Then those superstars played as a team and followed the instructions of their manager.

When we hire we always look for people who work well with others. Work habits and history are important. They don't even need restaurant experience. We can teach them The Chick-fil-A Way.

When Operators interview potential team members, they look for a good general appearance—how they're dressed and groomed, and whether they appear to be taking care of themselves. I'm impressed when an applicant has already begun earning money by cleaning yards or doing other jobs around the neighborhood. Labor laws make it difficult to hire people under sixteen; I was well on my way to my destination when I was thirteen years old. Even though boys and girls can't work for us that early, they show initiative when they find other ways to earn money.

We have a saying around the office, "An Operator gets the people he or she deserves to have." Good people attract good people. Even in a tight labor market some Operators say they have a waiting list of people wanting to come to work for them. Customers have observed the operation, they like the people they see behind the counter, and they want to associate with those kinds of people. A few Operators have a more difficult time hiring good people, and we have to remind them that they are getting only what they deserve. Once you get them, you motivate them so that they enjoy their work. We have T-shirts that say, "It's fun to work at Chick-fil-A." Have fun and get the job done. The more people enjoy their work, the more likely they'll be productive and stable.

Then there's one other element that comes into play: Most folks here feel that this is more than just a job. They feel either a divine call or the satisfaction of a desire to make a difference in the world. Our people contribute to their communities in ways they could not if they were associated with any other company. They feel a sense of significance.

They contribute greatly to the development of teenagers who work in our restaurants, creating a wholesome atmosphere in which to work and modeling positive leadership traits that teenagers will take into their adult lives. Our Operators consider themselves to be mentors to the next generation.

I RECEIVED A LETTER FROM A CUSTOMER who said she was having a bad morning when she came into Chick-fil-A. The teenage employee cleaning the coffee machine greeted her, then said, "You look sad."

"I am sad," the lady responded.

"Ma'am," he said, "you're too blessed to be stressed."

Hearing those words from a young boy, the woman said she woke up and realized she had more blessings than she deserved, and she wrote to tell me about it.

Teenagers also see how character traits, positive and negative, can be magnified in the work environment. I know of one girl who wanted her boyfriend to work with her in one of our restaurants, and she prevailed upon the Operator to hire him. After a couple of days, however, she recognized that his work habits did not measure up to the Chick-fil-A standards, nor did his language and attitude. Working elbow-to-elbow, she learned, is a great place to evaluate the character of an individual. Everything is beautiful in a convertible on a moonlit night. You can't see the flaws in the dark, but the workplace shines a bright spotlight. She got rid of him.

NOTE TO PARENTS OF WORKING TEENAGERS: You can share in your children's experiences of stepping out into the world for the first time. Picking up a child after work at night offers a wonderful opportunity to share. Teenagers are much more open to talking about their day or evening at work at that moment before they settle down from being so active in the business. If you wait until later, when they have moved on to something else, you may lose the chance.

If you want to hear from your children, you have to make yourself available at their initiative, not yours. You may say, "Let's sit down and talk," and find your child has nothing to say. You have to spend time together in a relaxed atmosphere, and then they will open up to you.

When our daughter, Trudy, came home from college, she told me the thing she remembered most about me as a father was when I came to her bedside and let her tell me what she had done that day. I would have thought she would remember the clothes we bought for her, our house, or other material things. But those things were secondary to her. The most important thing was my time.

THE PEOPLE WE HIRE AT CHICK-FIL-A CAN PERFORM many of the tasks required of them immediately after training. But there's an art even to scooping Waffle Fries or cole slaw if you want high production.

Nell Reynolds, a team member in Lubbock, Texas, holds the record for scooping the most cole slaw in half an hour. She is so smooth she hardly loses a drop getting the slaw into the cup and snapping the lid on.

Others are especially adept at checking chicken for bones

and preparing it for cooking. I observed one young lady, though, who was taking a full minute to bread a piece of chicken. I appreciated her care, but she could have done the job just as well in much less time. Operators must be aware of the time their team members are taking for each task. Those working too slowly might not have been properly trained, coordinated, and challenged.

Some Operators can run the restaurant with 5 percent less labor cost than others because the team is productive and light on their feet. They desire to do the job as quickly as possible.

While we place a high priority on swiftness of foot when evaluating potential team members, a positive attitude is much more important. One of my greatest pleasures is receiving nice reports on employees. And the compliments come often. Some people even go to the trouble of writing to tell me, for example, that they were shopping, had several bags to manage along with a couple of sacks of Chick-fil-A products, and an employee stepped out from behind the counter to help them to the car. It makes an impression on people when we do those things that are not expected of us. We hope all employees understand the importance of their jobs as ambassadors of Chick-fil-A. We want them to represent the chain well.

We also want them to perform with a good attitude when they're out of the customer's sight. Everyone from the Operator to the newest hire must be willing to do any job in the restaurant: prepare food, wash dishes, mop floors, clean restrooms. I was the janitor at the Dwarf House, and it's still my job to pick up paper on the floor, or whatever else needs attention. Team members should take it upon themselves without being ques-

"I look for ways to do special things for customers."
Rudy Martinez, San Antonio, Texas

I carry a stack of $10 movie rental gift certificates in my pocket, and whenever I catch an employee doing something special, going the extra mile, saying something special to a customer, I pull out one of those certificates and give it away. And I always try to do it in front of the rest of the team so the person's good deed will serve as an example. They never know when I'll pull it out.

On Saturday, when I have a lot of high school students working, it's a great incentive. They see somebody win one at eleven o'clock, and they say, "I'm going to win one by two." Then they start looking for ways to do special things for customers all day. It's a lot of fun.

I look for ways to do special things for customers too. Like when I see customer three or four times in the same week, I go to their table and give them a "Be Our Guest" card. I figure if they're spending fifteen or twenty dollars a week, I'll give them a free sandwich. Or if I see a family with children eating their Kids Meals, I might go to their table and put down a free Icedream for each of the kids. Parents love that. Then they're not just customers, they're loyal customers for life.

All of this fits into the Chick-fil-A philosophy that I first experienced when I went to work for the company at age twenty eight. I thought I was living before I came to work at Chick-fil-A. But after I became involved with this family, I'm living in a completely different world. I have friends working for other restaurant companies who burn out after a few years. Their companies don't care about them or their families. Just money. I was happy as a minimum-wage team member who couldn't even speak English, and now I'm happy as an Operator because I know everybody in the company cares about me. Happiness is not the money I earn here. It's in what I'm doing— the people I'm helping, the people I'm loving, and the people who love me.

tioned to keep the restaurant shipshape all the time. Of course, Operators must demonstrate how to do each job well. For many of our customers, a clean restroom is a sign that we keep the areas that are unseen just as clean. Jeannette and I have been in restaurants where we both found the restrooms so dirty we decided we should probably eat somewhere else.

Our Operators train team members to clean restrooms the way they expect them to be cleaned. If you're in and out in five minutes, that's not a clean restroom. When top executives demonstrate that they don't mind doing the dirty jobs, team members understand that every job is important.

Walking through the food court at a mall, I look for restaurants that are neat and clean, where people behind the counter appear professional, are in uniform, and appear eager to serve the next customers. People often tell me that they stood in line at Chick-fil-A while workers at nearby restaurants sat behind the counters reading a book, not giving any attention to their business.

When a Chick-fil-A restaurant Operator coordinates personnel, purchasing, and sales, and the team provides super service to their customers, that restaurant can generate more revenue per square foot than almost any other type of fast-food restaurant in the country.

WE HOPE CUSTOMERS VISITING ANYWHERE IN THE COUNTRY know the Chick-fil-A Chicken Sandwich they order will taste just like the ones they eat back home. Few things are more important than consistency in the food business. Customers want no surprises. We give them what they expect when they come in—consistent quality.

It doesn't cost any more to make a perfect chicken sandwich. We use the same boneless, skinless chicken breast, the same breading and seasoning, the same pickles, and the same bun. It's the human element involved in preparation that makes it different. But we have found a recipe that customers prefer, so we do it the same way every time in every restaurant.

Occasionally a team member will surprise an Operator with a new way of preparing one of our products. Like the kitchen worker who took the Operator back and showed him the purple cabbage she had used to make slaw.

"Doesn't that look pretty?" she asked.

It may have looked prettier to some, but it's not what the people are accustomed to at Chick-fil-A. So the Operator threw away all the slaw, made it according to the recipe, and told his team member, "Don't put any more purple cabbage in the slaw."

I learned that lesson years earlier at the Dwarf House. At breakfast the grill man buttered the toast with a pastry brush, cut it in half, and put it on the plate. I thought it would be a good idea to let the waitress cook the toast in a toaster, then put it on a plate with a wedge of butter. We could free up the grill man and make the whole operation more efficient. Well, from the customer backlash you would have thought I had told them to cook their own breakfast. They wanted their toast cut in half and buttered before it came to them. We had to go back to the original way of doing it because customers required it.

Customers don't like surprises.

CHAPTER TEN

Crisis and Purpose

A brief period in the history of Chick-fil-A, 1980–82, may have been the most severe ever for the company. By 1980, times had never looked better for the company. We had opened 100 locations and were experiencing impressive same-store sales growth. The nation was becoming more health conscious and was recognizing the benefits of chicken over beef. A sharp increase in the price of beef in 1979 precipitated price increases for hamburgers, and even more people came our way.

For thirteen years we had grown our business in a virtual greenhouse. No other major quick-service restaurant chain had succeeded in a national roll-out of a chicken sandwich product, although according to reports, McDonald's had tested several, with little success.

The 1980s were referred to by some as "the malling of America," and our commitment to opening new restaurants in mall locations positioned us perfectly for growth. Our plans

Above: A bronze plaque with our Corporate Purpose sits outside the front door of Chick-fil-A headquarters.

called for an additional 100 restaurants by the end of 1981—
we would double in size in two years. To accomplish that feat
we recognized the need for more brain power. We needed help
with the marketing, real estate, and legal aspects of the company.

My son Dan had been working in the corporate office for
seven years, along with Jimmy Collins and Perry Ragsdale, who
designed all of our restaurants. Buck McCabe came to us in
1978 from Peat Marwick, our accounting firm, to handle our
finances. My younger son, Bubba, had also joined the Executive
Committee.

Even with 100 locations, we were a small company in
many ways. We ran the Chick-fil-A business out of a growing collection of offices in Hapeville. In 1967 we had bought
an air freight building on Virginia Avenue for offices and
warehouse space. As we hired more people, we squeezed
warehouse space tighter until we ran out of room. We brought
in a mobile home and converted it into additional offices,
and when that wasn't enough, we bought two neighboring
houses. Soon we ran out of space again, so we leased offices
in a building a mile away. We were squeezing people into
every corner we could find. Jimmy Collins, who was then
executive vice president, worked for thirteen years in that
former air freight building in an office without a window.
When Buck McCabe came on board, we didn't have an office
for him at first. His desk was our lunchroom table, so every
day at lunch he had to put away his work so we could all
gather around to eat together. (I had finally stopped working
the lunch rush at the Dwarf House every day by then.)

We continued to bring on talented people to help us grow.
Bureon Ledbetter, a recent top law school graduate, came on

board to handle our real estate and legal affairs, and Steve Robinson, formerly Director of Marketing at Six Flags Over Georgia, took over our marketing operation.

With those additions, we had the brain power to take the company to the next level—to double our size over the next twenty-four months. We also made plans to move and consolidate our offices in a single headquarters building.

In 1980 I learned about seventy-five acres of beautiful hardwood forest adjacent to Interstate 85 south of Atlanta that had been in foreclosure for seven years. I had been looking for property for three years, so I knew Atlanta real estate well. The price for such a large tract just four miles from the airport seemed unbelievable. I drove over to see the property and discussed it with my real estate agent. It was true. I immediately pictured our headquarters building nestled among the trees, in a setting only God could create. The architect designed a plan that took advantage of the setting, with many windows and balconies and a skylight atop a five-story atrium. After we opened in 1982, the *Atlanta Business Chronicle* cited our facility as one of the six most beautiful corporate headquarters in metro Atlanta.

We spent close to $10 million to build our headquarters— a vast sum considering the size of our company and the capital needs required by our tremendous growth at the time.

THEN INTEREST RATES HIT 21 PERCENT—not on the long-term loan for our headquarters, but on construction costs for our 100 new restaurants. The high cost of borrowing money slowed mall development nationwide. Five malls had been scheduled to open but were delayed by the developers for months. Four were delayed for nearly two years. Other malls were opening with only half their spaces occupied, severely limiting the potential traffic in our restaurants.

Perhaps even more significant, two of the huge hamburger chains finally decided to enter the chicken market. In April 1980 Wendy's added a chicken sandwich to its menu. McDonald's later followed with Chicken McNuggets. Those two monoliths went toe-to-toe in their battle for market share, with Wendy's airing its memorable "parts is parts" television commercial.

All of that focus on chicken would be good for us in the long run, but the immediate effect was a double-punch that caused me many sleepless nights. Our competitors were buying so much chicken that suppliers began to be squeezed, and the cost of breast meat soared. The consumption of so much breast meat created a secondary problem for suppliers—what to do with the wings, legs, and thighs of all those chickens. Wings were not yet the rage, and poultry producers had no market for half of every chicken they grew. That loss forced them to raise prices on breast meat even further. Double-digit inflation hit every other area of the business as well, from utilities to taxes to wages. Then in 1982, we had our first and only decrease in same-store sales, even as we were adding more restaurants. Add to that mix the mortgage on a brand new $10 million headquarters—which began to look like a $10 million tombstone—and the emotional strain on me grew heavy. I didn't know how high expenses would rise, or how low sales would slide. I fought the temptation to increase our prices, knowing the move would reduce our volume.

Raising prices for me has always been the absolute last resort—after we squeeze every bit of waste we can. In 1982 I felt the squeeze myself. I took no salary. I believed it was a necessary step for the long-term good of the company, and I didn't want anyone else in the company to have to take a pay cut. Everything I owned was wrapped up in Chick-fil-A. My name was on every note, and it wasn't hard for me to envision a total loss.

I spent many days and nights in prayer that year asking God, "Where have I failed You?" The downturn in the business, I believed, was a result of my actions or inaction. I prayed for His correction, then I shared my concerns with my family and the Executive Committee.

I have told my Executive Committee many times that I can deal with any problem except a financial problem. I'm a product of my upbringing, living from hand to mouth for so many years in the boarding house. Our family was so near the edge of bankruptcy throughout my childhood that I had vowed never to risk that possibility as an adult. And even though Chick-fil-A never missed a payment, a continued downturn in the economy could have led to deep financial trouble. And, as Jimmy Collins said, "Truett's the only one of us who can't just go out and get another job."

In October 1982 I scheduled a two-day meeting of the Executive Committee to review where we had been, project where we were going, and chart a course for getting us there. Everyone working for Chick-fil-A could see the same negative business trends, and I think they probably expected us to come back with a blueprint for success. In the back of my mind I might have had the same expectation. I asked the Executive Committee members to bring all of their numbers, charts, graphs, and projections.

We isolated ourselves for two days at Pine Isle Resort on Lake Lanier, north of Atlanta, so we could avoid the distractions of the office. There we analyzed the company, the industry, and the economy inside and out, and after hours of discussion we determined that we were operating the company responsibly, the economy runs through cycles, and the current climate was not a permanent situation. In other words, we found ourselves no closer to a solution than when we had started. We finally had to ask ourselves what we hoped to accomplish in two days.

At that point my older son, Dan, asked more basic questions: "Why are we in business? Why are we here? Why are we alive?"

My first response was to put aside such questions and stick to the matter at hand—our difficulties in the business and our response to those difficulties. We had a business to run.

But Dan was not being rhetorical. He really wanted us to consider the purpose of Chick-fil-A, and he believed the answers to his questions might lead us to solutions to our more immediate problems as well. So the eight of us began something of a brainstorming session, putting ideas on a blackboard as we went.

The discussion quickly focused on our individual priorities. We were unanimous in our belief that each of us wanted to glorify God in all we say and do. It was only natural that we would also want to glorify God through our work.

Discussing God's role in our lives was nothing new to this group. More than fifteen years earlier, at our original office near the Dwarf House, three or four of us had begun weekly devotional times on Monday mornings. The tradition continued and grew as the company expanded and moved into our new building, and our Executive Committee members attended regularly.

But our devotional time focused on our personal relationships with God. We had not addressed the role of Chick-fil-A in those terms.

My style has always been low-key with regard to my religious convictions. I hope that people see something attractive in the way I live that leads them to seek the One who leads me. In my own personal way I had committed the company to His purpose but had not done so publicly.

It became obvious that the Committee was moving toward doing just that. By the end of the day we had developed two statements, which became Chick-fil-A's Corporate Purpose:

To glorify God by being faithful stewards
of all that is entrusted to us.

To have a positive influence on all who
come in contact with Chick-fil-A.

We returned to the office, and the staff asked us what we had decided.

"Well, we don't have a solution to the problem at hand," I said, "but we did establish this as our Corporate Purpose."

(We had, in fact, addressed the more immediate situation after we committed our purpose to paper, outlining a new promotional program and an internal campaign emphasizing the importance of quality, service, and cleanliness. We knew we were the best in our market. Everything we did had to enhance our superiority.)

The following Christmas the employees gave me the huge bronze plaque with the Corporate Purpose inscribed on it. I'm not one to put up a lot of signs, and I wondered where the best place would be to display it. Someone suggested putting it by the front door to remind each of us of our purpose when we come into work.

Some companies will make a statement like that, then put it in a desk drawer and forget about it. Having the plaque out front has kept the Corporate Purpose alive for us. It certainly has been a good reminder for me.

For example, I sometimes find myself pretty careless in my telephone conversations. A man from New York called recently and told my secretary that he needed to talk with me about a personal matter. She put him through, and he greeted me like a long lost friend. Then he said he wanted to talk to me about investments.

"You're talking to the wrong person," I said. "You need to talk to the vice president of finance."

"No, I want to talk to you," he insisted, and he rattled on.

Finally I'd had enough, and I interrupted him saying, "You were very rude to my secretary, and you were not truthful with her in getting your call through to me."

He continued on, and I hung up.

Instantly I was aware of our Corporate Purpose: "To have a positive impact on all who come in contact with Chick-fil-A."

Since that day I have tried harder to have positive impact on callers like that man as well as other people who have created difficult situations. When we make that effort, I believe, the result is a positive influence on each of us.

WONDERFUL THINGS BEGAN TO HAPPEN in the months following our adoption of the Chick-fil-A Corporate Purpose. We experienced 28.9 percent growth across the company in 1983, a tremendous follow-up to the same-store sales decreases we had seen a year earlier. Significant unexpected opportunities outside the operations of the company came our way, leading to the creation of the WinShape Centre Foundation and the chance to shape winners.

More important, I felt confident in the future.

Occasionally parents ask me to talk with their children about a difficult issue or to help them mediate a disagreement. A father and son were in a dispute over the son's use of a car, and the father asked me to talk to the boy.

"What's the trouble?" I asked the son.

"Dad got mad at me about something, and now he won't let me drive the car. It's sitting there in the driveway, and I feel like an idiot when my friends see it sitting there and I can't drive."

"Have you ever thought about giving the car away?" I asked.

"What?"

"That's right. If you give that car to God, it's no longer yours to worry about. You take care of it and drive it, but it's His car. Do that and you'll have a totally different feeling about it."

"Yeah, maybe," he said.

We called his father in, and the son told him what I had suggested. I had to explain the concept to the father as well.

I was not in a position to follow up on that father and son to see how they worked things out and whether the boy followed through. But when we established our Corporate Purpose, I was reminded that I had given Chick-fil-A to God. I operate it and take care of it along with our staff and Operators, but it's His business. When I remember that, I have a totally different feeling about it.

Chapter Eleven

Building Boys and Girls

Instruction is what we say.

Influence is what we do.

Image is what we are.

Not many men can claim that more than 150 children call them "Grandpa."

It's my proudest distinction. Our three children have given us twelve wonderful grandchildren who will be growing into adulthood in the next few years. One of Jeannette's favorite lines when she's talking with them is, "Grandmama's praying for you. Be sure you make good choices." Each of our natural grandchildren has unique gifts and abilities in academics, art, writing, athletics, and music. Dan, Bubba, and Trudy are doing a beautiful job of preparing them to step out into the world as responsible citizens.

But millions of other children across the world do not have

Above: Some of Truett's favorite times with his foster children are spent doing little things.

the advantage of two committed, loving parents. Fifty years ago I chose to teach Sunday school to thirteen-year-old boys because it is such a critical age—perhaps one of the last opportunities to make a lasting impact before they make decisions that will permanently affect their lives. Over the years many children living in difficult home situations have come under my influence.

I enjoy bringing boys from Sunday school out to our farm for an afternoon or for dinner. Many of the boys who come have been in some sort of trouble and need more positive influences in their lives. I might give them a chance to earn some money cutting grass or doing other projects around the farm. When our own sons were growing up in the 1960s, these troubled boys would work shoulder to shoulder with them. Then over dinner we talked about the consequences of poor choices.

Dan says today of those discussions from years gone by, "I was eight or nine years old, and I saw these boys who were four or five years older than I was. The folly of their decisions and the fallout from them saved me from making a lot of foolish decisions myself. Some of them were defiant, disobedient, or using alcohol. They had very destructive forces in their lives." The unintended but positive consequence was that these boys were object lessons for our own children, who later avoided trouble.

A few years later, when Trudy left home for Samford University in Birmingham, Jeannette and I found ourselves in an empty house. Dan was at Georgia Southern University in Statesboro, Georgia, and Bubba was at Samford University in Birmingham. Their leaving created a void in our home. I like to have people around, especially young people. So if I had a Saturday to spend around the farm, I continued to invite some of my Sunday school students—not just the ones who were in trouble—over to ride trail bikes.

It was about that time that a boy, Woody Faulk, attended my class for the first time. Woody's parents had divorced when he was four years old. His father worked for a securities firm, and his mother held two jobs to earn enough money for the family. Similar circumstances have crushed many boys. But not Woody. He had demonstrated his leadership abilities by becoming one of the youngest Eagle Scouts in Florida.

He was on a Scout trip when word came to him that his mother had been killed in an automobile accident. His grandparents were dead, and his father had not been in contact for years, so Woody was sent to live with an aunt and uncle in a suburb south of Atlanta. They brought him to my Sunday school class, and I soon became aware of his situation. I immediately noticed his high standards and capabilities, and I didn't want the loss of his parents to become a burden he could not overcome. He visited Jeannette and me at the farm several times, and I asked him at one point to let me see his report card. He said later that I was the first man ever to ask him about his schoolwork. Knowing someone was genuinely interested, he made straight A's from that point on.

Jeannette and I grew to love Woody and wanted him to become a part of our family. Our children agreed that adopting Woody was a good idea, but his mother's will would not allow it at that time. When he graduated from high school and enrolled at the University of Georgia, however, he became like an adopted child to us, moving his things into the guest room in our home and staying there whenever he came home on weekends.

When Woody graduated, I told him I hoped that he would come to work with Chick-fil-A, but he had to make up his own mind on that. He did join the company, and he is now Vice President, Brand Development. When Woody and his wife, Rae, married, he asked me to serve as his best man. They now have three daughters of their own.

Getting to know Woody as a teenager, I came to understand even more clearly that a lot of children who have never done anything wrong, who are not involved in drugs, alcohol, sex, or violence, can be a victim of their circumstances. They have a lot of potential, but no opportunities for that potential to blossom.

When these children enter my life, my natural instinct is to be generous—to give them whatever it would take to make them happy. But following through on that instinct could lead to dangerous consequences.

I was driving in Florida when a sixteen-year-old girl driving a red Mustang convertible ran a stop sign and plowed into the side of my Ford F-150 pickup truck, shoving me into a telephone pole. Both doors of the truck were jammed shut, and I had to force one side open and squeeze out. The Mustang was totaled. Luckily, neither of us was hurt badly.

I've reflected on that incident often, thinking about the joy that father must have had in giving his daughter that car, and the joy she had in receiving it. But the father didn't take into account what could have happened. He didn't use common sense in turning over that little car to his sixteen-year-old girl. His poor judgment might have cost him his daughter.

I experience tremendous joy in giving, but I also try to be sensible about it.

My joy comes in seeing children grow up and make something of their lives.

In 1983, I was invited to speak for two days to business classes at Berry College in Rome, Georgia. I had grown up in Georgia and had heard of Martha Berry and the school she founded, but I had never visited the campus. When I arrived I drove through the gates of the college, which Miss Berry eighty years earlier had dubbed "The Gates of Opportunity."

The more I learned about Martha Berry, the more inspired I became. She was born to a well-to-do family in 1866 and grew into a beautiful young woman with plenty of suitors. She easily could have lived a life of leisure.

Then one Sunday afternoon Miss Berry walked over to her favorite reading spot, a log cabin near the Berry home. As she read she sensed someone was watching her. She looked up and saw three barefoot boys looking at her through the window. She invited them in and asked a few questions. Her biography, *Miracle in the Mountains*, describes the encounter:

> Where did they go to school?
>
> "Ain't got no school. They was one o t'other side the ridge, but it's fer boys livin' thetaway beyon' the gap."
>
> Martha went on with her questioning. "Don't you go to Sunday school, either?"
>
> The tallest boy stared. "What kin' of school?"
>
> "Where they teach you about God and Jesus."
>
> The three were more surprised than ever. "They's somethin' to learn about 'em?"
>
> "They tell you Bible stories, too."
>
> "Oh, we 'uns got a Bible, on'y Pa cain't read it."

So Martha Berry immediately began to tell the boys stories from the Bible—exciting stories of David, Samuel, and Abraham, and they begged for more. Then she gave them ginger cakes and invited them back the following Sunday. There would be more cake, and lemonade too, if they would wash their arms and hands every day of the week.

Sunday after Sunday they returned with clean hands and more friends, and Miss Berry knew she had to do more. Over time she envisioned and established a boarding school for the mountain children who otherwise would have grown up uneducated. In so doing, she followed the admonition of her father regarding assistance to others:

> "The people around us so often need help, child. But how to give it the wise way—that's the question. If you simply hand things to somebody you destroy his pride, and when you do that you destroy him. Let him take charity and he comes to expect charity. If he gets a bag of flour the first time, you have to give him another on the second visit, and the third time he'll look for more than that. But if you can lend him seed and tools and let him make his own crops, he'll keep his self-respect. . . ."

Although destitute, students did not attend Martha Berry's school for free. They had to work on the adjoining farm to generate income for the school. In each of these children, born into circumstances that might have led to the same life of poverty their parents lived, Miss Berry saw a spark of promise that she nurtured and fanned until it became a flame of hope.

As I drove through the campus she had built, I noticed that every building had a spire on it, even the barns. Some had several spires. I later learned that Martha Berry insisted on the spires so the students would always be led to look to God.

After speaking to the business students at Berry, I invited Dr. Gloria Shatto, president of the college, to speak at our Airport Rotary Club. In our conversation she told me that the Berry Board of Trustees had decided to close the boarding school for grades five through twelve. It was costing $2 million a year to keep it open, and they could not justify the loss any longer. She invited me to come up to see the facility and perhaps offer an idea for its possible use.

Jeannette and I drove up and found a beautiful Mountain Campus, with a magnificent chapel rising up on a hill, stone dormitories, library, classroom building, gymnasium, and administrative building—all sitting idle. It looked like a postcard of a New England campus, and it was beginning to show signs of deterioration because of disuse. Something had to be done to make use of this beautiful place.

(A member of the Chick-fil-A Executive Committee once said, half-joking, that they sometimes "hide" real estate from me. If our company buys a site with an old building on it, they don't tell me about it because I don't like to tear anything down. I hate to see anything go to waste, and would rather figure out a way to make use of it. This is a sad analogy—one that sometimes breaks my heart—but we have children across our city, our nation, and our world who are going to waste because the adults around them think they're useless.)

Jeannette and I talked about what Martha Berry had done almost a century earlier at that spot—bringing children out of the nearby mountains and teaching them. A plaque at the campus explained that this was where it began:

> This campus was an integral part of Martha Berry's educational vision. From 1916 to 1983 it was the site of the Mountain Farm School, Foundation School, Martha Berry School for Boys, and Berry Academy.

We prepared to leave the Mountain Campus and drive to Dr. Shatto's office—it was about three miles through the woods to the main Berry College campus. Before we got in the car I asked Jeannette what she thought. "I feel like I'm standing on holy ground," she said. We both felt immediately drawn to the place—as if we had been called to it.

Over the next few hours sitting with Dr. Shatto in her office, a vision began to unfold in my mind and heart. I described to her the inspiration: housing for Berry students who would receive scholarships from Chick-fil-A; a foster home for promising children who otherwise might not get a chance to succeed; a summer camp for children. All these things would fit right in with Martha Berry's mission—and our mission at Chick-fil-A. Dr. Shatto loved the idea and anticipated approval by the Berry Board of Trustees.

Jeannette and I returned to Atlanta, and the next day I met with the Chick-fil-A Executive Committee to describe what I had seen and experienced. They responded politely but did not encourage me. I think they saw this as a huge salvage job that would turn into a black hole and suck away cash that might be invested in other worthwhile projects. I took the Committee, along with my pastor, Dr. Charles Q. Carter, up to Berry so I could show them the campus and let them see the vision for themselves. Jeannette, I believed, had assessed the situation correctly: Berry was holy ground, for God had sanctified it for His purpose. I wanted the Committee and Charles to see that purpose. But when they saw the buildings, they did not see the vision. Rather, they were impressed by the Berry College Board of Trustees' decision to close the Mountain Campus because it was a $2 million annual drain on their budget. Every one of them believed it would be a mistake to take on a project of such magnitude, and they told me.

I knew, though, that God was in it. This undertaking was bigger than anything we could ever do alone—in fact, we would surely fail without His active and direct involvement. And because He was with us, the vision for the Berry Academy campus was destined for success. With God's leading, we could not fail. We proceeded, calling our vision WinShape Centre, "shaping individuals to be winners."

The first step, we believed, was to reopen the dormitories. Dr. Shatto said we would need at least fifty students, so we started figuring out what it would take to get fifty students up there. We immediately created a scholarship program, offering a $10,000 four-year scholarship for each worthy student. Chick-fil-A paid half of the scholarship, and Berry paid the other half. We promoted the scholarship program across the nation, primarily targeting high school students working for Chick-fil-A restaurants.

College scholarships were nothing new at Chick-fil-A. Eleven years earlier we had begun offering $1,000 scholarships to worthy team members who worked with Chick-fil-A.

Sixty-eight students with WinShape Centre scholarships of $10,000 started at Berry in fall of 1984, thirty-four boys and thirty-four girls. At this writing, in 2002, we have 125 students on the Berry scholarship. We've twice raised the scholarship grant, which now is $24,000 per student, to meet rising tuition costs, and still divide the cost equally between Chick-fil-A and Berry. Since the inception of the WinShape Centre, nearly 780 students on scholarship from WinShape have attended Berry.

I love to visit the campus during the school year when students fill the place with life and excitement. When they go home for summer, though, the campus they leave behind falls silent. Part of the vision for WinShape Centre was a summer camp for children.

Talk about a place coming to life! More than 1,600 campers from across the United States and two foreign countries attended Camp WinShape in 2001. The summer is divided into several two-week sessions. Hundreds of campers come from urban areas, where they have never before walked in the woods, or gone outside at night to look up at a starry sky without the orange glow from nearby streetlights.

The camp program is designed to guide the children in their moral, spiritual, and physical growth. Many of the campers—including any member of my Sunday school class—attend on a 50 percent scholarship provided by Chick-fil-A, and some children attend free. All of the children in our U.S. foster homes attend camp.

I like to tell the kids at Camp WinShape, "You have a 28,000-acre playground." The Berry College campus, the largest in acreage in the world, is also one of the most beautiful.

WE ALSO BUILT OUR FIRST FOSTER HOME at Berry College's Mountain Campus, and an entirely new dimension opened in my life.

To establish a home for children we needed three things: a home, parents, and children. Which comes first? Rather than spend a lot of time creating master plans and long-range forecasts, we depended on the Lord to lead us in our decisions. I contacted Harry Brown, whom I had taught in Sunday school many years earlier. He and his wife, Brenda, were now house parents at Christian City while he continued to work at Southern Bell, and I asked him to keep an eye out for children who might be appropriate for our foster home. We also informed schools, churches, and caseworkers for the Department of Family and Children's Services of our facilities and capabilities.

Then one day Harry called and said he might want to operate a Chick-fil-A restaurant. I asked if they would like to be house parents at our foster home instead, and he said yes. He and Brenda were willing for him to take early retirement from Southern Bell so they could do it. The Browns were older than I had expected our house parents to be; I anticipated young parents full of energy and excitement. But I had seen them interacting with the children at Christian City, and I knew first-hand of their deep, abiding faith. They came on board at Berry and over the years filled the lives of more than 100 children who came through their home with love and devotion.

Recently Harry wrote and reminded me of the permanent impact adults can have on the lives of children: "If it had not been for you, I would not have been interested in changing the lives of children. Because you cared about me over forty-five years ago, I decided to try to be a father like my Heavenly Father instead of one like my earthly father."

For Harry and Brenda and many other foster parent couples in our homes, their work is a ministry, taking on the role of natural parents for up to twelve children. If it were nothing but a job, the weight of that responsibility would soon crush them. Nobody has the stamina to do it for more than a few months. But if the Lord has called them and anointed them for this, the desire will be great within them, and they will experience a strength and stamina that they cannot explain.

Our house parents stay with us an average of ten years, long enough to provide a stable home for children to grow up and leave for college. This is one of the keys to the success of our foster homes—to stop the revolving door.

Different children's homes are created and designed to meet the needs of different types of children. The children at the Paul Anderson Youth Home, for example, have been in serious trouble with the law. Christian City Home for Children seeks to reunite children with their natural parents, and they gear their programs toward that end. We seek a third type of child. Our children have not been in serious trouble with the law, but they usually have parents who will never be able to take them home again.

When we opened our first home, I thought I would have to screen the whole United States to find twelve children who would fit into that category. We soon found, however, that they were right in our own community.

We used an interview process to help determine who would be appropriate for our home. I might ask, for example, "Have you ever been sent to the principal's office?"

The child would answer, "Once or twice."

"What for?"

"Talking back to the teacher."

That kind of trouble would not disqualify a student from our foster home. But if he said, "I hit my teacher in the face with my fist," he would not be a candidate for us. You put that child in among nine good children, and you will soon have ten troubled children.

We were looking for good children with potential to be winners but who would not have a chance without our program.

A caseworker once told me, "You just want the good kids."

"Yes, that's exactly what we want," I said. "You have other programs for drug addicts, alcoholics, and children with sexual abuse problems. But where are the people who will take those who haven't been in trouble, those who want to be winners despite their circumstances? We do our best to attract those kids."

As the caseworker reminded me, all of these children are troubled to some extent. You don't come from the environments they have been exposed to without damage. We understand that.

Our homes provide the best permanent alternative for many children. We offer the stability, love, and discipline they have never experienced. Our goal is a permanent relationship with children. We don't want our children to be taken away from us to be adopted into other homes. They are as precious to us as our own children, even if they are not legally "ours."

Unfortunately, state and federal laws prohibit long-term foster care and push for adoption. It is discouraging when a child who has lived in the same house for several years, who calls me "Grandpa" and the house parents "Mom and Dad," sees his picture on an adoption poster in a restaurant. Our house parents have adopted several children themselves, and I have become legal guardian of others to keep them from having to leave.

Reuniting a child with his or her parents is inappropriate when you have a fifteen-year-old boy going home to his mother, who is living with her twenty-one-year-old boyfriend who doesn't even have a job but suddenly wants to be the boss of the household. That situation will quickly deteriorate to the point where the child will be living on the street if you don't get him out.

I stood before a Department of Family and Children's Services panel that was determining the fate of one of our children and asked, "Does it matter that the mother lives first with one man and then another?"

"Mr. Cathy," the chairman responded, "it matters to you and it matters to me, but according to the law we can't discriminate. As long as the parents furnish a roof over their head and food on the table and clothes on their backs, we can't separate the child from his mother simply because she has men friends."

The problem with these mothers who have live-in boyfriends, besides the horrible home situation they present, is that many of them would give up their children instead of the stragglers.

In this case, the mother wanted to keep the boy *and* the boyfriend. They lived in my community. I had bought Christmas gifts already, and I called the mother to ask if I could bring them.

"They're already wrapped," I explained.

"Well, I don't know about that," she said.

Then her boyfriend got on the phone and said, "I wish you'd just leave us alone. We don't want those gifts. You do whatever you want to with them."

The gifts stayed in a closet in our home for several years, and were a reminder of this child.

A couple of years later the boy called me from jail. He had gotten married and, because he did not want to keep his mother's name, had taken the girl's last name. They had divorced and he wanted me to help him in a rough situation. We often continue relationships with children whether or not they're in our care.

The responsibility of overseeing our foster homes demands considerable time, and many days I find myself focusing more on the children than I do Chick-fil-A. I thank God that I am not in either endeavor alone—that He has provided talented and dedicated people to help shoulder the responsibility.

School groups often come by the office. A big group of kindergarten children was spread out on the carpet in front of my desk, and I asked them what they wanted to be when they grew up. The answers included the usual: fireman, policeman, doctor, preacher . . .

Then one boy spoke up and said, "When I grow up I want

to be a zookeeper."

Well, then all of the children began to reassess their career choices, and after that every one of them wanted to be a zookeeper, zookeeper, zookeeper.

"Gee, I wish I had thought of that a long time ago," I said, "getting paid for playing with the animals."

Another little boy kept his hand up and insisted on telling me what he wanted to be.

"Yes," I said, "what do you want to be?"

He looked at me and said, "When I grow up, I want to be like you."

Wow. That struck me deeply. I don't know what triggered that thought in that six-year-old boy whom I did not know, but for some reason he had been prompted to say he wanted to be like Truett Cathy. I picked him up in my arms and said, "This is the highest compliment I have ever received."

And in a case like that I have to be very careful about what I say. More important, I have to be very careful about what I do.

You never know how and when you influence people—especially children.

CHAPTER TWELVE

Moving Beyond the Malls

Several factors in the mid-1980s led us to consider the possibility of building free-standing Chick-fil-A restaurants. Mall development across the country slowed dramatically, and some mall developers were not keeping their facilities fresh with the times. They were losing major tenants, which meant we were losing potential customers. About the same time people began to tell us through our research, "We'll eat at Chick-fil-A more often if you make it more convenient." They didn't care to go into a large mall just to eat with us. They wanted to park close to our entrance, or even use a drive-thru window.

In 1984 we asked Tim Tassopoulos, currently Senior Vice President, Operations, to oversee the operation of our free-standing restaurants. This was not a totally new concept to us—the Dwarf House was nearly forty years old at the time and more successful than ever. But it was a new way of thinking for the Chick-fil-A business.

Above: Chick-fil-A free-standing restaurants are designed to be recognizable by their silhouette even in moonlight.

Until then we had not dealt with structural engineering, exterior signs, parking lots, and landscaping. Perry Ragsdale, Senior Vice President, Design and Construction, had hoped to develop a single set of architectural plans that would work for any location. We soon found, though, that it wouldn't be that simple. There were too many variations in lot sizes and zoning codes. We maintained a standard "look" of our restaurants, however, by creating a shape and an overall image that is recognizable as Chick-fil-A by moonlight, with all the lights off.

We moved deliberately, opening our first location in Atlanta in 1986 and slowly expanding our presence in other markets with free-standing restaurants and making good decisions each time. Initially one of the most difficult issues was securing strong sites. Since the early 1960s, fast-food chains had developed many of the best locations. We were a latecomer to the scene. That situation may have worked to our advantage, however, ensuring that we investigated every opportunity thoroughly before moving ahead.

Our capital requirements also ensured deliberate growth. I am conservative in the amount of money I will borrow to build new restaurants. I also prefer to own the real estate under our restaurants rather than to lease. The initial investment is greater, but when the loan is repaid, the advantage is clear. I've owned the Dwarf House since 1946 and haven't made a note payment in decades. For nearly twenty years as we located in malls, owning real estate had not been an option.

Our physical requirements differ from other restaurants; we require more interior space because of our commitment to preparing food fresh on site. In our first eleven free-standing sites we built basements for dry storage, which allowed us to build on smaller lots. But we soon found that soil conditions and other factors made that arrangement inefficient.

In 1993, after successfully opening forty-one free-standing restaurants, we opened our first drive-thru-only location. We knew we had terrific drive-thru products that we could deliver quickly and that people could eat without ruining their clothes.

We decided to try our first drive-thru-only in Greenville, South Carolina, where we had not opened any free-standing restaurants. Near the parking lot of McAlister Square Mall we built a small drive-thru with two windows, designed to do about $750,000 worth of business per year. Well, the first year we did $1.4 million. Cars were lined up across the mall parking lot and backed up down a four-lane highway.

The Operator had done a tremendous job through the years serving customers in the mall and had created a pent-up demand for our product.

We quickly added a twenty-three-foot extension to the drive-thru, giving us more space inside for faster production so we could take care of more customers. All of the subsequent drive-thru-only facilities have taken advantage of our early experience.

In the twenty-first century, mall development has virtually halted, and all but a few of our new restaurants are free-standing or licensed restaurants in nontraditional markets.

In the early 1990s, we created a Business Development Department to investigate new ways of delivering Chick-fil-A products to new customers. They helped develop our catering and school delivery programs as well as a mobile Chick-fil-A restaurant that travels to large events.

The Business Development Department also recommended

that we contract with food service companies to make Chick-fil-A available on college campuses, in hospitals, and at other locations where a traditional restaurant might not be an option. The benefits were immediately obvious, and in 1992 we opened our first licensed restaurant on the Georgia Tech campus in Atlanta. We now have nearly 200 licensed restaurants all over the country, and we're opening about twenty more every year. We're also in airports, a hotel, and office and bank buildings.

The licensed restaurants differ from our traditional locations in that Chick-fil-A contracts with large food service companies such as Aramark, Sedexho Marriott, and Compass to build and operate Chick-fil-A restaurants through a licensing agreement. We ensure our high level of quality by contracting with a nearby Chick-fil-A Operator to be responsible for training the management at the licensed restaurant and checking on the operation at least weekly.

Specifically, one of the greatest benefits of serving Chick-fil-A on college campuses is our exposure to young adults who will become our customers of the future. With 11 million transactions annually and growing, that's a lot of positive experiences, which lead to a lot of loyalty.

As WE ADDED FREE-STANDING RESTAURANTS, WE ALSO introduced Chick-fil-A Kid's Meals to our menu as a service to parents who had their children with them. Chicken Nuggets and Waffle Potato Fries, two products pioneered by Chick-fil-A, made a meal that kids enjoyed.

Very early we distinguished our Kid's Meal by including a prize that reflected our values. We have offered books on history, geography, weather, plants, animals, and dozens of other subjects. Stories on tape have helped children learn the importance of establishing certain character traits. And with interactive educational cards, kids have enjoyed English, social studies, geography, math, and science. Parents, if they decide to, can use the prizes as tools to teach their children or help instill character values. Steve Robinson, Senior Vice President, Marketing, and his department developed the program, which now offers eight or more series of collectibles every year under the theme "Growing Kids Inside and Out." *Restaurant Hospitality* magazine has named the Chick-fil-A Kid's Meal the "Best Kid's Menu in America" for the quick-service food category two years in a row.

Positive response from parents to our Kid's Meal prizes, as well as the nation's growing concern for school children's character development, led us to expand our education component. Chick-fil-A now sponsors Core Essentials, an educational program available nationwide designed to give teachers and parents the necessary tools to educate elementary-age children about character and values. Developed to teach children about values such as honesty, cooperation, and responsibility, the Core Essentials program covers twenty-seven values over a three-year period. With this program it is as though we've gone full circle, back to my own high school days and my favorite class, Everyday Living.

Our focus on children also led us to build playgrounds—some of them indoors—at many of our free-standing restaurants. The attention to our younger customers is paying off, as Kid's Meals now account for 6 percent of our total sales. We believe the positive experience will lead these children to become lifelong customers of Chick-fil-A.

"We're creating a family atmosphere."
Marla Davis, Dayton, Ohio

I want anything said in front of my customers to be something I would be proud for a three-year-old child to hear. We're creating a family atmosphere—a place where we never worry about what the cashiers or anybody else behind the counter says.

Developing that atmosphere begins with the interview process. We always create role-play scenarios to see how potential employees would handle various situations. We learn whether they can think for themselves and react appropriately to an irate customer, and whether they're service oriented.

Sometimes during an interview I will "accidentally" knock a stack of papers off my desk and see if the interviewee will pick it up. If they're service oriented, they'll immediately reach down for them. If not, they'll hesitate or wait for me to pick them up myself.

Our restaurant is near a major entrance to the mall, and during lunch we get a lot of business people who want their order quick and right. They're not interested in a lot of conversation. Just smiles.

Those peak periods can be like a game for us. We see the wave of people coming, and we're prepared for them. We cook out front in our restaurant, so the customers see how fast we're working for them. It's hurry, hurry, hurry, then it slows for a few minutes before the next wave pours in, and we get right back at it.

Jeannette and I found our latest challenge in Florida. There aren't many restaurants where she and I would stand in line for an hour to get a table, but Marko's, on Highway 1 in Port Orange, Florida, was one of them. It was our favorite place to eat when we visited the area.

Marko's was family owned and started out as a small curb-service restaurant on a corner lot. The owner lived in a house a few feet behind the restaurant.

Over time the restaurant grew, he converted his menu to fine dining, and customers waited in line to eat with him. He expanded several times, incorporating his house into the restaurant and adding even more dining rooms, until he had a 15,000-square-foot conglomeration with halls and rooms in every direction, and people couldn't wait to get in. Nobody served better food, and everybody knew it. The place was an institution.

Then the owner retired and sold Marko's to a man who changed some of the features customers had loved best. In time the restaurant went bankrupt and closed, and for years every time Jeannette and I drove by, we wished we could do something to bring it back to its original glory.

We got our chance. Marko's went on the auction block with four acres of land, the building, and equipment. I made an offer that was well below what the bank was willing to sell it for, and Marko's sat empty for another year. Finally, though, the bank called me and said they would accept my offer.

We considered holding the property as an investment rather than trying to reopen Marko's, but I enjoy a challenge. And what a challenge it has been!

Jeannette and I got in there with the carpenters, electricians, and plumbers doing the physical labor necessary to prepare

Marko's for the public. The work was a lot like it had been fifty years earlier when my brother Ben and I built the original Dwarf Grill . . . except Marko's was ten times bigger.

We found plumbing problems, and all of the add-ons through the years had created a building code and operational nightmare. We learned that the city of Port Orange had strict regulations regarding lighted signs, and we could not advertise the restaurant the way we wanted to. We had to install a huge, expensive grease trap to comply with city ordinances, and we even had to get approval for our landscape plan. All of those regulations took some of the fun out of the work, and I was happy to have the Chick-fil-A real estate and design and construction departments available to guide us through the maneuverings.

I was also glad Jeannette was in there with me. She has a wonderful eye for design, and she decorated the whole place. Because of the restaurant's proximity to Daytona Beach, I suggested that we go with a racing theme. We brought in NASCAR and Indy race cars, along with antique motorcycles and other decorations. On opening night we let motorcycle riders eat free.

Like all of our restaurants, we close on Sunday. And we do not serve alcoholic beverages. These two decisions run contrary to the expectations of any resort-area restaurant or banquet hall, but we are not willing to compromise our principles in any situation. One party reserved the restaurant for 120 people, then called back two days later and canceled because the group wanted alcoholic beverages. But other groups appreciate the environment we are creating and have booked parties with us.

We are building success one loyal customer at a time, and we make sure that everyone who comes in leaves with the intention of coming back.

CHAPTER THIRTEEN

Bring in the Cows

When we made a commitment in 1986 to build free-standing restaurants, we knew we eventually would have to become more active in conventional media. Potential customers wouldn't walk by free-standing restaurants by the hundreds the way they did our mall locations, so standing out front with samples and other point-of-sale marketing techniques wouldn't work. Instead, we would have to drive transactions by educating people about who we are and what we stand for. This would require a new marketing approach.

We could not change our approach overnight. We still had more mall locations than free-standing restaurants, plus, we didn't have enough restaurants in any single market to justify expensive television advertising.

By the 1990s, however, we had enough free-standing restaurants in a handful of cities to warrant the help of a national advertising agency with significant creative abilities. Our mar-

Above: The Cows have become ambassadors for Chick-fil-A on billboards and as popular plush toys.

keting department selected The Richards Group in Dallas, Texas, a company with a history of creative success and a tremendous leadership team committed to our business. As our marketing team brainstormed with them, we asked, "How can we compete with the hundreds of millions of dollars other quick-service restaurant companies are spending on advertising—primarily on television, the most expensive medium?" We needed a less expensive way to stand out from the crowd.

The Richards Group recommended that we dominate billboards in our markets. At that time quick-service restaurants used billboards to push low-price promotions or to give directions, telling drivers to "Turn Here," or "Stop Next Exit." Billboards were rarely utilized in establishing an identity.

The Richards Group convinced us that we could build brand support quicker with billboards than we could with a limited television or radio campaign. Then they suggested that we use three-dimensional artwork, which was then a relatively new technology used primarily around theme parks in California and Orlando.

The first billboard they designed in 1995 showed a huge 3-D rubber chicken stretched out across the top with the line, "If it's not Chick-fil-A, it's a joke!" It was located at a major interstate exchange in Dallas. We liked the billboard and the results it generated, and asked The Richards Group for more. Later they presented our marketing team with another package of ideas. Our Senior Vice President of Marketing, Steve Robinson, recalls finding six different layouts on his desk, facedown, early one morning in 1995. Greg Ingram, our Senior Manager of Creative Services, had left them for Steve to review.

"Standing at my desk, I flipped them over one by one, left to right," Steve said. "There were several cute ones among the group that I liked. Then I got to the end, and there were these two Cows, one sitting on top of the other, painting a board in their scrawl, 'Eat Mor Chikin!' "

People down the hall could hear Steve laughing when he turned over that last layout. He immediately recognized its potential and got the support of the Atlanta Operators to put it up on a huge billboard on Atlanta's major interstate highway near the Atlanta Braves' stadium. The overwhelming attention from the public, and even the media, prompted us to quickly put up billboards in all of our top twenty-five markets.

As soon as the Chick-fil-A Eat Mor Chikin Cows appeared on billboards in these markets, customers came into our restaurants talking about them. The media quickly picked up on them, and radio talk shows and traffic reporters starting joking about them.

Then in the summer of 1996, some Chattanooga teenagers stole one of the Cows, and the national media responded. CNN, and even Court TV, picked up the story, as did hundreds of newspapers and other TV outlets, generating a ton of free national media coverage. We decided not to press charges against the young "Cow-nappers" upon the Cow's safe return.

That one billboard concept had succeeded beyond any of our expectations, and our marketing department challenged The Richards Group to take the Cow idea and develop an entire campaign around it, keeping it fresh, relevant, and entertaining. According to Don Perry, our Vice President of Public Relations, the Cows have generated the equivalent of millions of dollars worth of media coverage and publicity since the inception of their campaign.

The "Eat Mor Chikin" Cows now have become more than characters in an advertisement. They're real. Wherever I go I

"A key to success is community involvement."
Richard Gonzalez, San Antonio, Texas

One of the most important things we do for our customers is make sure we are fully staffed during peak periods. I'm amazed when I visit other restaurants (not Chick-fil-A) and find only one or two registers open and several others sitting idle. We spend the dollars to stay fully staffed so that customers will be served fast by friendly people.

Having enough people on hand also ensures that our employees can count on help on their left and their right if they need it. That makes even the busiest times more fun.

Another key to success in our little corner of the world is community involvement. If somebody calls and asks for something, we give them something. And if churches and schools don't call us, we call them and make the offer.

We've made contact with practically every school in our area. We are one of many Chick-fil-A restaurants with a Unit Marketing Director who coordinates our efforts in the community. She makes a tremendous difference in our exposure, often planting seeds for the future by getting involved in children's events. She may present an award at an elementary school, and bring the Cow mascot along. (Actually, the Cow makes the presentation, and the kids love it.) Then every child in the school gets a "Be Our Guest" coupon for Icedream, and the top ten students get meals.

It seems the more we give to our community, the more customers support us.

carry a bunch of plush Cow toys. They always make people happy, whether they're children or adults—even workers in boots and soiled shirts. Everybody loves them. When I give one away I always ask the person to tell me what the Cows say, and hold onto it until they say, "Eat Mor Chikin!"

What better way to get people to associate fun with Chick-fil-A?

In his book *The Peaceable Kingdom*, Stan Richards, founder of The Richards Group, tells of the broad impact of the Cows campaign: "One consumer wrote to tell us the campaign was so effective that every time he sees a field of cows he thinks of chicken. We co-opted an entire species."

With that in mind, the Cows—with help from The Richards Group—wrote *The Chick-fil-A Moo Manifesto*, which states in part:

> The Cows always act in a renegade manner. These aren't your garden variety Holsteins. . . . They know if they don't continue to surprise us, they become boring and expected. Which is one step away from becoming burgers.

> The Cows have a fairly simple sense of humor. They don't believe in elaborate productions. Theirs is a "grassroots" effort, so they always opt for the simplest, most economical way to get their point across.

> The Cows can't spell. Oh, they give it their best shot. But cows aren't the smartest creatures in the world, especially when using someone else's language. Their grammar isn't so hot either.

THE COWS REMIND US THAT WE'RE NOT LIMITED to traditional media for advertising. Some of the strongest messages can be delivered for free. I carry a big Chick-fil-A shopping bag whenever I travel, and when I walk through the airport terminal or ride the tram to the concourse, someone invariably will say to me, "Oh, we love to eat at Chick-fil-A."

Immediately I have generated an unsolicited testimonial that usually has been heard by several people standing nearby.

I might respond by asking, "What do you like best at Chick-fil-A?"

Sometimes they say something like, "I love your chicken salad," and the conversation widens.

"I didn't know you have chicken salad," another person will say.

Many times people who wouldn't otherwise know who I am see the bag and commend us for Chick-fil-A Kid's Meals or our commitment to close on Sundays. Parents tell me their children sometimes don't understand why we close on Sunday, and it gives them an opportunity to explain that Sunday should be set aside for worship and family. Many of these conversations occur in the midst of a crowd, and our message gets passed on. That's one-on-one brand building, which can be the most effective.

I encourage anyone associated with Chick-fil-A to carry one of our big shopping bags. I tell our Operators to fill it with plush Cows and to be ready to give one to anyone who says, "Eat Mor Chikin!" It's a wonderful way to introduce our product, and you'd be amazed at how many people want one. I went to see my doctor and gave away Cows while I sat in the waiting room. When I left, three nurses came running down the hall, chasing me and saying, "We didn't get a Cow!" They didn't want to be shortchanged.

I give away thousands of them every year and consider it a great investment. For the cost of 100 Eat Mor Chikin Cows I get more positive response than any newspaper advertisement. I am convinced that the Cows' campaign and the awareness they have generated have contributed tremendously to our continuing same-store sales increases. The Lord has given us powerful tools to stimulate our business. If we keep the Cows fresh, they can be our icon for years to come. They're memorable. They're fun. And people look forward to the next billboard.

Since 1997 the Cows have also had their own calendar. In 2001, customers snatched up 900,000 copies of our "Cows in Sports" calendar, featuring the Cows participating in thirteen different sports ranging from traditional baseball, football, and basketball to platform diving, snowboarding, and synchronized swimming.

"The Cows trained day and night for months in preparation for the production," Steve Robinson told the media when a "Cows in Sports" calendar was unveiled. "Seriously, the Cows and their quirky antics have become a key symbol of Chick-fil-A's marketing communications and advertising programs. The calendars are yet another medium by which the Cows are spreading their important self-preservation message to 'Eat Mor Chikin.'"

More than 1.25 million "Cows to the Extreme" calendars went out in 2002, featuring Cows in thirteen different extreme sports, including bungie jumping! The Cow Calendars, priced at $5 each, included more than twenty dollars' worth of Chick-fil-A food coupons with a different coupon offered each month of the year. The calendars have become so popular that schools, churches, and other organizations have ordered large quantities of the calendars to use in fundraising activities. We also made them available in our restaurants and on our Web site. In fact, we gave 72,000 copies in less than twenty-four hours as part of a promotion on our Web site during the 2000 Chick-fil-A Peach Bowl broadcast.

The "Cows in Sports" theme is a reflection of our involvement in the sports arena. Since 1995 we have sponsored the Chick-fil-A Charity Championship, a Ladies Professional Golf Association (LPGA) tournament held in Atlanta and hosted by Nancy Lopez. The following year the chain signed on as the first-ever title sponsor of the Chick-fil-A Peach Bowl, the classic college football match-up between Atlantic Coast Conference (ACC) and Southeastern Conference (SEC) teams. These two events have already raised more than $3.5 million for WinShape Homes and other charities.

Plus, they have greatly raised the awareness level of Chick-fil-A. In 1998, I suggested that we give away a Cow plush toy to every person attending the Chick-fil-A Peach Bowl—more than 73,000 of them. Some folks wondered whether that was a wise investment, at a cost of several dollars each. But unlike other "premiums" I've seen given away at other events, all of the Chick-fil-A Cows went home and continually reminded people to "Eat Mor Chikin!" Additionally, throughout the game a motorized flying Cow blimp made its way around the inside of the Georgia Dome, occasionally dropping a plush Cow to the fans during breaks in the action on the field. Some fans were watching the Cows more than the game itself.

CHAPTER FOURTEEN

Making a Difference

I received a letter in November 2000 from Michael Brown, a Chick-fil-A Operator in Augusta, Georgia. He said, in part:

> . . . Sometimes as an Operator it is easy to get bogged down in the day-to-day activities and lose focus on the real reason I got involved with Chick-fil-A. I am partnered with Chick-fil-A because I want to make a difference. I want to be a business mentor to my employees, and I want to show our customers that there is an alternative to poor quality food and even lesser quality service.
>
> When people ask me what is the secret to our success, I tell them that the recipes could be duplicated, but no one has. I tell them that the outstanding service that we give could be duplicated, but few companies have. I

Above: Jimmy Collins, who retired as President and Chief Operating Officer in 2001, believed, "Encouragement is the most important thing I do."

tell them that the overwhelming quality of our team members could be duplicated, but no one has. I believe the reason Chick-fil-A is so successful is simple—we care much more than our competitors.

Being successful requires doing more than just unlocking the doors every day. Our philosophy of "doing the right thing and doing things right" is hardly ever the easiest solution. It is, however, always the best solution.

Truett, I want to thank you for always "doing the right thing" and caring so much. The Chick-fil-A business philosophy is infallible and is undeniably the reason that we have the blessing of God. I am proud to be a part of the Chick-fil-A team, and you have in me a loyal protector of the brand.

Before Michael joined us he had prepared himself for success by earning a master's degree in business. He researched our company long before he approached us asking for an opportunity for a franchise, and he realized the potential we could offer one another. But the greatest potential he saw was in the difference he could make.

Michael did not realize how timely his letter was, for even as I read it at my desk, our staff was planning our 2001 Chick-fil-A Seminar, which would carry the theme, "Making a Difference."

Every year we take all of our Chick-fil-A Operators and their spouses to a resort location for a four-day business seminar that promotes the vision, values, and culture of our company. The Seminar has been described as a pep rally, a family reunion, a spiritual retreat, and a business refresher course. We bring in outside speakers like Zig Ziglar, John Maxwell, Lou Holtz, Ken Blanchard, Crawford Loritts, or Dennis Rainey to address our group of more than 2,000 on leadership, personal development, and business development. Our Executive Committee members update Operators on various aspects of the business.

In 2001 my pastor, Dr. Charles Q. Carter, opened our Seminar, as he has for the previous twenty years. Charles spoke on the difference we can make in the lives of others, focusing at one point on the importance of our personal example:

> We impact others by the life they see in our routine as we live. If I were to ask who won the last five World Series or the last five Super Bowls, few people in this room could name them. Or if I asked who won a Pulitzer Prize or a Nobel Peace Prize, you probably could not tell me.
>
> But if I ask you who are the three persons in your life who have influenced you the most, you can name them one, two, three. Who are the teachers who stimulated you and challenged you to be academically your best? You can name them just like that.
>
> The lesson is that you don't have to make the headlines to make a difference. You can make a difference by impacting others around you by the life you live day by day.
>
> Last week I was having lunch with two outstanding leaders from Georgia, CEOs of large corporations. I mentioned that I would be here in Orlando to speak to the Chick-fil-A family, and the theme of your Seminar this year is "Making a Difference." One of the men, Frank, spoke up and said, "I can give you a great illustration of that: the Chick-fil-A Operator in my hometown in North Carolina. No person in that town has made a greater impact than that Chick-fil-A Operator, who has been there

for many years.

Later Frank sent me a message identifying several areas where this one individual had been involved in civic activities, social activities, his church, and around the world—and especially touching the lives of young people, not only those who were Chick-fil-A scholarship winners, but touching the lives of some who were on the wrong path. This Chick-fil-A Operator, by his personal life and example, got them turned around and going in the right direction.

You can make a difference by personal example.

HUNDREDS OF THOUSANDS OF TEENAGERS will work as part-time employees of Chick-fil-A restaurants at one time or another. Operators can make an indelible impact on each of them, giving them skills they can carry for life if they are properly trained. Operators can help their employees establish good permanent work habits and attitudes. We talk about our responsibility to get every order right for every customer. We also must get it right every time with our employees. One day soon, they will be adults in the business world, and even if they're not with Chick-fil-A, we want them to have fond memories of having worked with us.

To continue making a positive impact on the people around us, we must avoid complacency in all aspects of our lives. The dictionary defines *complacency* as "self-satisfaction accompanied by unawareness of actual dangers or deficiencies." Too often we see people who are satisfied with mediocre performance and minor achievements. They look next door and see that they are doing as well as their neighbor. At work their accomplishments rank right up with the national average.

But look at what it means to be average. You are the worst of the best and the best of the worst. You're not achieving anything unusual, choosing instead to go with the flow. When we do less than our best, we become discontent and "burned out." Occasionally, I will have an Operator offer to terminate the franchise agreement with the explanation, "I'm just burned out on the restaurant business."

"Are you performing at your best?" I ask.

"Not all the time," comes the invariable answer.

It is when we stop doing our best work that our enthusiasm for the job wanes. We must motivate ourselves to do our very best, and by our example lead others to do their best as well.

People like to follow those who are excited about their work, not workaholics. It's tremendously rewarding to see children who have grown up with parents running a Chick-fil-A restaurant now working with Chick-fil-A themselves. One father with a restaurant has three sons who operate Chick-fil-A restaurants. We also have daughters of Operators now running their own restaurants. That's a high compliment to parents, and evidence that the parents brought home good reports of their experiences each day. It's often difficult to balance family and business needs. A parent often must work on Saturday when children are involved in soccer or baseball games. But the restaurant schedule also offers flexibility to Operators after the lunchtime rush to be involved in family and community activities. We invite spouses to our annual Seminar to remind them of their integral role in the success of the restaurant and of our commitment to their family. The only thing worse than having an Operator die, I believe, is for one to experience divorce. So we strive to find ways to support the family.

That level of enjoyment has been a key in leading us to the

"Every flat period is temporary."
Mike Edmonds, Annapolis, Maryland

The day I say, "This is as good as it gets," is the day we begin our downward slide. I will never say we have tapped out our growth or believe we can't put more over the counter. We can always sustain more growth. Always. Even in December, when we did $310,000 in twenty-four days and people asked how we could get that many people through the restaurant, I knew we could do even more. And we will.

Occasionally we will have a flat month or two, or even be down in sales. It's easy in those times to blame a softening economy or a reduction in mall traffic, and then believe we've peaked. But the day we do that is the day we begin our descent.

Every flat period is temporary, and we'll be growing again soon.

I came to Annapolis in 1996 and was tempted, as most Operators are, to develop a business plan to promote our restaurant. But that's backwards thinking. We have to build a great operation before we can go out and promote it. That plan is based on Truett Cathy's model in dealing with people—trusting them with opportunities they may never have had, identifying ability and potential, and matching the right skills to the right job.

I've found that if I take care of my people, they will take great care of the customer. It sounds so simple, but the biggest key to our success is being consistently friendly with our customers. People come in here and have their favorites on the day team, and they don't want anybody else to wait on them. They've developed friendships, and they can count on each other. That's the model of giving we've all experienced at Chick-fil-A—giving to the customer at the counter, and to the community.

$1 billion mark in sales. In 1989, our Executive Committee established the $1 billion sales goal by the year 2000, and I have to admit I didn't like the idea of such a lofty, long-term target. The year we set the goal we had 415 restaurants and total sales of $271 million. My attitude regarding the distant future is to do the best we can every day and take advantage of unexpected opportunities. That combination will lead us to success. I don't want to set some arbitrary target out there that might lead us to make inappropriate decisions just to achieve it.

But my son Dan said, "Dad, would you agree that we can achieve a 12 to 15 percent sales increase over the next eleven years?" The number, which would require 3 percent same-store increases plus a manageable number of new restaurants each year, was reasonable, so I went along with the plan. And I'm glad I did! We actually surpassed the goal in 2000 by $86 million, and now we're setting new targets.

COINCIDENTALLY, THE SAME YEAR WE ESTABLISHED our $1 billion goal, I was presented with the Horatio Alger Award. Named for the author who wrote 123 rags-to-riches novels, the Horatio Alger Association of Distinguished Americans was established by Dr. Norman Vincent Peale. Awards are presented annually to Americans from humble backgrounds who have achieved success in their respective fields while demonstrating a strong commitment to community service and assisting those less fortunate than themselves.

The Horatio Alger Association offers scholarships and other educational opportunities for young people. Association members also meet twice yearly, and through these meetings and my service on the Association's board of directors, I have come to know many of our country's most successful, inspiring, and philanthropic leaders. From Atlanta alone, members include Hank Aaron, J.B. Fuqua, Donald Keough, John Portman, John Rollins, Wayne Rollins, Herman Russell, Red Scott, Deen Day Smith, Wes Cantrell, and Ted Turner.

The common theme I have found running through each of their lives is this: A person can achieve anything if he or she has the right amount of "want to."

OUR ANNUAL SEMINAR GIVES ME THE OPPORTUNITY to address all of our Operators and remind them of our successes, both business and personal. And sometimes the personal successes are the most dramatic. I began having eye problems; I couldn't read a newspaper, and I feared I might lose my vision completely. My doctor suspected the problem was related to my mild diabetes, so I became more diligent in following the appropriate diet.

Then he sent me to a specialist, who discovered a blood clot at the back of my eye. "We can't fix it," he said, "but we can keep it from getting worse." I accepted his diagnosis, thankful that I could still see distances and would be able to continue driving.

Three months later, however, the same doctor examined me again and said the clot had moved. He didn't understand it, but he said he saw no reason why it would interfere with my eyesight any longer. But I still couldn't see close up, so he sent me to yet another specialist who said I had cataracts that were so small that removing them might do more harm than good.

All the time I was praying for God's providence—that He would work through the doctors to find a cure. Finally, I was sent to an eyelid specialist who noticed right off that I had droopy eyelids that were blocking my vision. He said it would be easy to raise them surgically.

"We can take care of those bags under your eyes while we're at it," he added.

So not only were my prayers answered with fully restored vision, but you can now see a more beautiful me. And that's good, at least for one woman who read the September 2000 issue of *Focus on the Family* magazine. The edition carried a wonderful article about our Corporate Purpose and the foster homes sponsored by our WinShape Centre Foundation. My picture appeared on the cover of the magazine, and shortly after its publication I received an eight-page letter from a woman who began, "I read the article about you in *Focus on the Family*. I'm not photogenic either." Maybe she'll see the new me on the cover of this book.

THE 2001 SEMINAR WAS MOMENTOUS in that Jimmy Collins, our president and chief operating officer, was retiring from the company after almost thirty-three years of service. Jimmy has addressed every Chick-fil-A Seminar, and in his final address to the Operators he offered strong words of encouragement:

> I'm not a natural encourager. I, by nature, am a critic. I see things wrong. A paper clip on the floor, a misspelled word on a sign. I have tried over the years to reinvent myself from a critic into an encourager. It's taken me years to realize that encouragement is the most important thing I do.
>
> It's also the most important thing Operators, parents, and staff do, too.
>
> So when I go into a Chick-fil-A restaurant I try to

catch people doing something right and make them an example. When I get a perfect chargrilled chicken sandwich, I take it back to the kitchen and say loudly, "I want to know who did this."

When someone steps up and says, "I cooked it," I say—in front of as many people as possible—"This is a beautiful piece of work. A perfect chargrilled sandwich. The bun is toasted just right; there's good bun coverage; the sear marks are perfect; it's not scorched or dried out; the pickles are just right, like you were arranging a party tray. You do beautiful work."

By that time a crowd has gathered around to see what I'm talking about, and not only has one person received well-deserved accolades, others have gotten a lesson in preparing a perfect chargrilled sandwich.

Jimmy followed his words of encouragement with a reminder that with good times comes hard work.

When I find myself in a position where I'm almost overcome by the amount of work necessary to accomplish a particular task, I like to remember a favorite scripture of mine, Proverbs 14:4: "Where no oxen are, the stable is clean, but much increase is by the strength of the ox."

In other words, if you want to enjoy the increase of the ox, then you're going to have to be prepared to shovel the manure. Obviously with more oxen, there's going to be more manure. As for me, I put on my gloves and my high rubber boots, and I'm in there digging with the biggest shovel I can find. How about you?

I hope your barn is so full of oxen you need a front end loader to shovel the manure. Hope we're swamped with business!

Then Jimmy reminded us of the core message delivered at the first Operators Seminar in 1971:

> Build the business.
> Guard the brand.
> Take care of your people.
> What counts in this business is not how much money we make or how much chicken we sell. What counts is the difference we make in the lives of others.

CHAPTER FIFTEEN

Making a Difference for Children

Nothing touches my heart more than to drive up to one of our foster homes and see the children come peeling out the front door yelling, "Grandpa's here! Grandpa's here!" then give me a hug and a kiss on the cheek. Ours is a relationship we have built over time.

Most new foster children spend at least a night, and usually a weekend, with Jeannette and me. We go out to eat, shop for new clothes, and spend lots of time getting to know each other. This is a special bonding time—often the most time an adult has spent with the child in years. I want each child in our foster homes to feel comfortable calling me Grandpa. One pattern I have seen among neglected children is that their clothes have been neglected as well, and the children know that. If we can get a few special things for them, along with baseball cards or

---

Above: Many of Truett's foster children join him for special events like the Chick-fil-A Charity Championship and the Chick-fil-A Peach Bowl.

other items they desperately need, we can often start breaking down barriers right away. We don't always have time to go to the store when we get the children for the first time, so I have bought a lot of clothes from stores that are going out of business or other special sales and I keep them, along with plenty of toys, in a storage area at our headquarters. Some of our staff like to call it "TruettMart." I just like to see the smiles when these neglected children begin to understand that somebody cares about them.

The government defines "success" for foster children as a permanent placement in a home. The state is so insistent in having children returned to their natural homes or adopted by a family that an agency will sponsor an all-day picnic so prospective parents can spend time with the children and decide if they want to take them home. If you like that boy and he's friendly, he can go home for the weekend with you so you can decide whether to keep him.

By experience, I've learned that adoption, although it sounds good, is not always the best alternative for children who are eleven or twelve years old and older. We had a group of three siblings who were separated because the youngest boy was adopted out of our care. We could have kept that sibling group together, which is important, but sometimes other plans prevail. Our house parents made every effort to keep them all together and were devastated to lose them.

Every time a child leaves I'm anxious to know how he or she is making out. I want to pick up the phone and call, but I can't. At the end of six months, the adopting parents have the choice of keeping the children permanently or "returning" them to the state foster child system. When these children come back into our homes, we have to start all over acclimating them to our expectations.

We had another group of three siblings who had been with us almost three years. They were thriving on the love and structure they had never known. An adoptive family was found that would take all three children, and the children left our home crying and devastated. Then the worst happened. The adopting family changed their minds months later and decided not to keep the children. We got a call asking us to take the children back but had already filled their places with other children. It was disastrous for everyone involved, and eventually the children were split up. We lost contact with three children we dearly loved.

The following stories will show you where some of the children in our foster homes have come from and how far they're going.

JENNIFER AND MICHAEL HAD BEEN LIVING WITH US for three years when their parents gave up all parental rights. The state wanted to put them up for adoption. I wasn't going to take a chance that we might lose these two precious children. They were well-adjusted, good children, and the trauma, the upheaval of a move to another family would have been devastating.

So I petitioned the state for legal guardianship of the children myself and was granted those rights. When the paperwork was completed, we had a celebration. I took them out to dinner, then we went shopping for a few special things at Wal-Mart. Afterward we went back home, and I asked them, "What do you want for dessert—hot chocolate, popcorn, or ice cream?"

"We want them all, Grandpa," they both said.

Well, you don't have too many nights as special as that one, so they got them all. Then they got themselves ready for bed, and we said our prayers together. Jennifer said she wanted me to rock her to sleep, so we sat in the rocking chair for awhile, rocking and talking.

Let me say here to any parent: If you don't have a rocking chair in your home, go buy one. I first saw its magic work in at the Carrie-Steele-Pitts Home in Atlanta before we opened our first home.

I asked the director, "How do you control discipline?"

"If they're misbehaving," she said, "I grab them by the collar, put them in my lap in the rocking chair, and say, 'Let me rock some of the meanness out of you.' "

The rocking chair sat right beside her desk. At Christmas I sent another rocking chair with a bow to her, and she called to thank me for it.

"Have you used it yet?" I asked

"Oh, yes, twice yesterday."

I've found that a rocking chair is good medicine for children who need discipline and loving. Most of the children in our homes haven't had an abundance of love expressed to them before they come to us, and they're anxious for it. I generally rock them when it's late and the house is quiet. The time together is soothing to me and to them.

While I was rocking Jennifer, this beautiful, freckle-faced, red-haired eight-year-old girl, I was explaining to her how she wouldn't have to worry about leaving—how I had become her legal guardian.

It was a difficult concept for a child to grasp, so I simplified it by saying, "This will always be your home, and we will always be here for you. When you're grown and have your own children, you can bring them back here to visit and always find your place here."

Jennifer seemed satisfied with the situation, and she fell asleep in my lap. I laid her in the bed.

The next morning at breakfast she said, "Grandpa, you're my guardian angel now, aren't you?"

I could feel the tears immediately well up in my eyes. "Yes, Jennifer," I said, "I'm your guardian angel, and I always will be."

Lives can be changed if we say the right thing at the right time with the right spirit.

Jennifer is growing into a beautiful young woman, and whenever we're together, I ask Jennifer, "Remind me how we're related?"

She'll smile and say, "You're my guardian angel."

Her title for me reminds me of both the joy and the responsibility of being a guardian. I must be careful in the things I say and do, letting her know that she can always depend on me. I must teach her about her personal responsibilities, and I must provide a model of goodness for her.

I WAS COMING HOME FROM A TRIP when I saw a sign for the Department of Family and Children's Services outside the courthouse in Murphy, North Carolina. I decided to stop and ask if they knew of any children in the area who might need to move into one of our foster homes. I went inside and told the woman in charge about our facilities and services and explained our goals for WinShape children. She called seven or eight caseworkers together and explained WinShape to them, and they said that a twelve-year-old girl named Janessa "really needed a break." She might be just right for WinShape.

"Would it be difficult to move her across state lines?" I asked.

"Let's go ask the judge," the woman said. "He's right around the corner."

The judge said he would have no problem allowing her to move to Georgia, and in thirty days we had a new resident at WinShape.

Janessa's house parents taught her many things from the Bible, among them the fifth commandment, "Honor your father and your mother, so that your days may be long in the land that the Lord your God is giving you."

Janessa picked up on the correlation between long life and obedience and wrote the following note to me on my birthday:

> You are truly a great grandpa, and I love you so very much. You must have obeyed your parents when you were young. Mom and Dad always tell us that if we obey our parents then we will live a long time. Well, I don't know if I'll live as long as you have, but I hope to have your character and personality. You love God so much and put him first in everything you do. I hope that I can do the same in my life. You are a great example for my family and me. Thank you for stopping in the little town of Murphy and taking the time to tell them about your "big family." You have given me great parents that I love so much and who care for me. Thank you! I love you!
>
> Your Granddaughter!!
> Janessa

The lesson Janessa learned from her house parents, respect for authority, is one of the most important ones we can teach children in our foster homes or in my Sunday school class. God tells us to obey our parents, and He tells parents to obey God. When you get a crowd of thirteen-year-old boys together in a room, they're going to wrestle, pick at each other, whisper to each other, and sometimes outright defy you. For years I thought this was a situation that I would have to live with as a teacher. But when I visited our foster home in Brazil, I went with the children and house parents to school and church. One woman who was with them asked the house mother, "How do you get ten children to sit there in church on those hard benches and listen to the preacher?"

"They don't have an option," the house mother answered.

Her words struck a strong chord with me. I came back and told my boys about those children in Brazil sitting on the benches listening to the preacher, fully attentive, and I told them what their house mother had said.

"From now on," I said, "you don't have an option either."

No longer did I stand in front of the class and say, "May I have your attention? Quiet down back there."

If a boy begins to whisper, I stop. When he realizes his mistake, he stops and I continue. They're learning respect for authority and our Sunday school lesson.

I DON'T MAKE A HABIT OF READING PERSONAL ADS, but something led me one day to flip through a PennySaver newspaper to see what people had written. I came across the following:

LOOKING FOR MAN. NICE TO LADY AND KIDS. ONE BOY 7 YEARS. ONE GIRL 9 YEARS. 28 YEAR OLD MOM FOR A LIFE RELATIONSHIP.

I thought about those two children, and a mother who would advertise in a newspaper for a man's help. She wasn't looking for a husband, but rather a "life relationship." From what I have seen, such relationships rarely last for a lifetime, and they often make a bad situation worse for children in the household.

This world is filled with so much need, and God specifically calls on us to care for orphans in their distress. These two children apparently were not orphans, but I wondered if there might be anything we could do to help them. I called the telephone number listed.

Without giving my name, I asked the mother whether her children's immediate needs were being met—if they had a place to live and food to eat. The mother—I'll call her Donna—explained that their father furnished a place to live, and she received $180 a month in welfare. I did not pursue the matter further at that time.

A month later Jeannette and I were back in Florida, and I picked up a PennySaver to see if the ad was still there. It was. I called Donna, and this time I told her who I was, and I asked her if I could bring her information about Camp WinShape.

"They're already enrolled in a camp with the Salvation Army," she said. "It doesn't cost anything."

"Our camp won't cost anything either," I said. "I hope you'll permit us to bring by some information."

She said okay, and Jeannette and I followed the directions she gave us to her mobile home. When we drove up, two children with smiling faces ran out to the car as if they knew us. We spent some time there getting to know Donna and the children, Chuck and Marcie (not their real names). When we felt that Donna was comfortable that we were who we said we were, we asked if we could take the children to dinner with us.

"They've already eaten," she said.

"What about tomorrow?" I asked.

She said that would be all right. When we came to pick up

the children, Donna met us with a camera and took our picture. Her continued concern for the safety of her children was obvious.

"If you're worried about the children," I said, "why don't you take our tag number too."

She did.

We began a relationship that night that continues today. Jeannette and I have shed many tears, in joy and in sorrow, for Chuck and Marcie, two children who so desperately needed stable adult role models in their lives.

We got them to Camp WinShape that summer, and almost every time Jeannette and I were in Florida we took them out to dinner with us. They were such sweet children.

They obviously did not have a good situation at home. Donna never found her "life relationship" and instead had a series of men come in and out of her life. After awhile she conceived a child and then found herself alone with three children. By that time, Chuck and Marcie were old enough to babysit, so Donna continued going to the local pub at night.

As Chuck and Marcie grew, they remained totally obedient to their mother. Even when he was sixteen years old, when I asked Chuck if he wanted to go somewhere he said he would have to check with his mother. But her influence was obvious, and her temper was evident. Once when she became angry with Chuck, she pulled the wiring from his car. She controlled her children with threats and intimidation, and they grew increasingly resentful of her.

When Marcie graduated from high school she immediately moved in with her boyfriend. Chuck, who was two years younger, set higher goals for himself. He wanted to attend Berry College. His teachers and school counselors recognized his obvious intelligence—he had a 3.78 grade point average—and they knew of the endurance test he was undergoing at home. They did what they could to support him.

Chuck continued to attend Camp WinShape each summer and spent additional time with our son Bubba and his family. We all loved him and Marcie, and we wanted them to do well.

But during the Christmas holidays when he was a high school senior, Chuck got mixed up with the wrong crowd at school. He got involved with drugs and started skipping school. Then he and some other boys drove to Tampa and broke into several cars. They got caught and went to jail. After he spent a few days there, I went down and posted a cash bond to get him out. I didn't want one mistake to cost him everything.

When he apologized and said he wanted to graduate, his teachers went overboard to see that he succeeded. Bubba and I urged him to finish his work, and he did, earning his diploma with his class. Although he remained on probation, he made plans to attend Shorter College in Rome that fall. (He had waited too late to get into Berry.) When school started he got a job at the Chick-fil-A Dwarf House in Rome, and everything looked good.

Then we started seeing evidence to the contrary. He started smoking out in his car. Then his grades came in: all F's except for an A in rope climbing. He involved himself with drugs again, and he was on the verge of flunking out of college. He acted as if nothing in the world mattered to him.

One night he took the car we had loaned him and told his friends he was going on a "three-day vacation." Knowing he was not supposed to take the car out of town, he drove all the way back to Florida.

I still didn't want to give up on Chuck. He had come too far in his life to lose it all in such a short time. So rather than report him missing and risk his arrest and revocation of probation, we found him near his home in Florida and got the car back.

Chuck then bounced around from one job to another, washing dishes or doing odds and ends. I went to see him one night at a pizza restaurant where he worked and asked him if he had any place to stay. He shrugged. I told him Jeannette and I had an extra bedroom, but he wasn't interested.

Since then he has wrecked a car, lost his driver's license, and has to ride a bicycle to work, where he has a job waiting tables. He has a second job at a theater. In the fall of 2000, he said he didn't want to see me anymore, so I kept up with him through his grandmother, and I prayed that someday we might be reconciled.

Then in April 2001, when Jeannette and I were in Florida, I stopped by the theater to see Chuck, hoping that we might have a few minutes to talk. I asked him if he would go with me to dinner at Marko's after he got off work at six o'clock, and he agreed. When I came back he hugged me, and for the first time in four years we sat at the table together. He apologized for his behavior, and said he had come to his senses. I continue to pray that we will be fully reconciled.

Marcie, in the meantime, has gotten her life in order. She graduated from dental hygiene school and is taking care of herself. She is concerned about her brother and his conduct, but isn't sure what to do for him.

April was eight years old when she came to live at our Rockhill foster home. Six years later, when given an assignment to write and present a speech, she chose me as her subject.

When I heard what she had written, I was so moved that I

sought several occasions for her to recite her speech. I saw the opportunity to strengthen her self-esteem, improve her speaking skills, and inspire her to dream big dreams. I also enjoyed hearing what she had to say about me.

April's speech focused primarily on my experience in the business world—selling Cokes as a boy, opening the Dwarf House, developing the Chick-fil-A Sandwich—and it was appropriate for a variety of business groups. The Newcomen Society, a foundation that recognizes achievement in American business, inducted me into its membership and invited me to address its members. I asked April to come give her speech.

April took a big step forward that night, addressing those business leaders as a fourteen year old at the prestigious Piedmont Driving Club in Atlanta. I listened again with tears in my eyes as she talked about "Grandpa." She wrapped up her speech by telling the group:

> Truett Cathy, the businessman, inventor, and benefactor, is not my real grandfather. You see, it is my privilege to call him Grandpa because I am a WinShape kid, sort of an adopted grandchild of his. I have learned from Grandpa the importance of hard work, practicing your beliefs, and helping others. I strive to be a granddaughter who will make him proud. I hope that by hearing some of his story today that you will be encouraged to be like my Grandpa. Thank you, and eat more chicken.

A CASEWORKER CALLED ONE DAY AND SAID SHE HAD THREE BROTHERS, ages twelve, fourteen, and sixteen, who needed a mom and dad. She hoped we might have a place for them. Unfortunately, we did not have three spaces in any of our homes.

"But I would like to be their friend," I said.

So I took the boys out to dinner, then to a store to buy them some clothes. Afterward we drove down to our foster home at The Rock Ranch, seventy-five miles southwest of Atlanta, to spend the night. We talked about all sorts of things, and sometime before they went to bed I read the third chapter of John from the Bible to them. In that chapter, Jesus explains to Nicodemus what a person must do to be saved. We finished the chapter, then prayed together, and they went to bed.

The next morning when everybody woke up, I told them I wanted to take them to breakfast at the Dwarf House. Driving up there, I asked the three boys, "Have you ever thought of becoming a Christian?"

"I already am a Christian," the older boy said. "I've been baptized."

The middle boy said he was a Christian as well.

"I'm not," said Nicholas, the twelve-year-old, from the back seat.

"When would be a good time to accept Christ?" I asked.

"Right now!" he cried.

Well, I had never had anybody answer that way before. Usually people will say, "Soon," or, "Next time I'm in church." Nicholas caught me off guard.

"You really want to become a Christian in the back seat of this automobile?" I asked.

"Yes sir."

"Well, if you believe that, close your eyes and pray a prayer I'll tell you. I'll keep my eyes open because I'm driving."

Then I relied on the song so many of us learned in church as children. "I want you to invite Jesus to come into your heart," I said. "Ask Him, 'Come in today. Come in to stay. Come into my heart, Lord Jesus.' "

Nicholas prayed that prayer, then I assured him, "That's all you need to do; let Jesus into your heart."

Nicholas beamed. A few minutes later at the Dwarf House, we saw Jumping Joe Ward, who had played basketball at the University of Georgia and with the Harlem Globetrotters. Joe, who is from Griffin, Georgia, now leads a ministry for young people.

He recognized me and came over to our table. He was sponsoring a youth meeting that night and had brought some of the Harlem Globetrotters into town for it.

He sat with us for a few minutes and I said, "Nicholas, tell Jumping Joe what just happened to you."

"I just invited Christ into my heart."

"Right here?" Joe asked.

"In the car."

"You mean in the backseat of that Lincoln? Praise the Lord, I'm going to share that with the group tonight."

The Williams boys were subsequently placed in a temporary foster home, and I lost contact with them. Then six months later I was speaking at a school, and afterward a boy walked up to me and introduced himself. It was Nicholas.

"Remember me?" he said. "I accepted Christ in the back seat of your car."

I knew that was a quick conversion, and I was not in a position to help him build on it. But when we have an opportunity, we have to respond to it as best we can and trust God to lead someone else into position to help.

So many times we have unexpected opportunities, and later we wish we had said something encouraging.

We recently had a thirteen-year-old boy, Stan, come stay in one of our homes when his mother was put in jail up in north Georgia. His father had been in state prison for several years in south Georgia. Stan was a smart boy, handsome and charming. He shook my hand and looked me in the eye when we talked. If you met him for the first time, you would say he was a leader in his school and would grow up to be a leader in his community. He had the look of a winner.

But after a few days in our home, Stan's house parents saw that he had become accustomed to lying to avoid responsibility. He took some things that didn't belong to him. He experienced the usual discipline, running a half-mile ring around the property a few times, or missing privileges like movies or ball games. After a few weeks he was beginning to understand what was expected of him and was getting along better with the other boys and girls in the home. All the while Stan adored his natural father, although he couldn't remember ever having met him.

Stan had been with us for two months when his father was released from prison and applied for custody of his son. The state granted that custody almost immediately and considered, I am sure, the case to be a success because a child had been reunited with a father.

In fact, Stan was headed toward disaster. Two months later the father was back at our doorstep with Stan at his side. The father's live-in girlfriend didn't want Stan around, and the father realized he was not capable of rearing a thirteen-year-old boy. When the father saw our foster home at The Rock Ranch, the home he had taken Stan from, he said, "I didn't have any idea it was this nice. I never would have taken him if I had known."

I don't know how this story will work out. In the two months that Stan was away from us, his father allowed him to do things we would never allow, and we had to start all over trying to establish some stability again. After that, Stan wanted nothing more than to run back to his father, whom he adores.

Stan's house parents are patient and loving, and they're giving him every opportunity to succeed. I, too, have spent time with Stan, encouraging him to direct his many talents toward the good. I build him up, reminding him of his athletic and academic talents. He looks me in the eye and says he wants to do right. Now he must fully convince himself of that fact.

ONE OF THE GREATEST REWARDS FOR ME as a foster grandparent is for children to grow up in a WinShape Home and dedicate their lives to becoming foster parents themselves. At least four children have made such a commitment.

Richard was thirteen years old when he came to our attention. He also had a younger brother and sister. Their mother had abandoned the family when Richard was four years old, and their father, who was blind and had behavior problems, subsequently gave up his responsibilities as well. Richard and his siblings lived with foster parents, and Richard continued monthly supervised visits with his father, whom he loved. The foster parents wanted to adopt the children, but they also wanted the children to sever all ties with their natural father. Richard was not willing to give up that limited contact, so he remained in the foster care system, moving to a different family.

I learned about Richard and wanted to meet him, so I coordinated with the foster parents to pick him up in nearby Conyers on a Saturday morning and take him to Rome to show him our foster home. We spent the entire day together in my truck, driving up to Rome and back. Richard told me some of the heart-breaking experiences of his childhood. This thirteen-year-old boy was on the verge of stepping into manhood without ever having had an appropriate role model. I shared with him the source of my strength in difficult times, and told him the promise I carried with me in my memory and my heart: "Seek first the kingdom of God and His righteousness and all these things will be added unto you."

I invited Richard to come and live in our foster home, and he accepted. I told him I wanted him to be my chosen grandson. Years later, he told me that my choosing him "made me feel extremely special. For you to bring me into your family and choose me was a great gift."

Richard became the first member of his family ever to graduate from high school. At his graduation party, I gave him a watch with his name and the date engraved on the back. Then I showed him a ring that was custom made for me.

I told Richard, "When you graduate from college, this ring will be yours."

Richard set his sights on college graduation—not so he could get a ring, but because he knew people cared about him, loved him, and wanted him to succeed. Four years later he graduated, and today he still wears the ring.

Richard wears a wedding ring as well. He asked me to serve as his best man the day he married Stephanie. And when their son was born they named him Samuel, my first name. That little boy is my namesake.

People ask me why I invest so much in the foster homes. The one thing I take more joy in than anything else in the world is seeing young people develop. They grow and make good decisions. They want to be winners despite the odds against them.

And all the while I enjoy a wonderful, loving relationship with them. I have been the best man in four weddings, standing up for young men who moved beyond their difficult family situations and are now important contributors to their own families and communities. Three couples have said they, too, want to be foster parents. They want to give back to others what they received as children. That's why I invest so much in these kids—because the rewards are so rich.

Richard and Stephanie told me they want to multiply their joy by serving as house parents. I suggested, however, that they wait. They have their own child now, and they're building the foundation for a lifetime together. They need this time together before pouring themselves into foster care.

I hope that in ten years the desire will still be there and they will fulfill that dream.

As our three children, Dan, Bubba, and Trudy, grew toward adulthood, one of my greatest fears was that one of them would fall in love with somebody from across the country and establish their home far from us. I couldn't bear to be away from our children and grandchildren. None of our children, though, had any intention of leaving the South. Dan and Bubba married and settled south of Atlanta near us, and Trudy, who lived in Birmingham for six years, met and married a fine young man, John White. After a few years in Birmingham, they moved to Atlanta, and we were surrounded by our growing family. We did not know, however, what plans God had in store.

While they still lived in Birmingham, John had told Trudy he felt God calling him into overseas missionary work. She replied, "If God's calling you, He's going to have to call me too, because we go together."

For several years the subject lay dormant as Trudy worked through her own call to missions. Then in 1979, while attending First Baptist Church in Atlanta, Trudy began to feel her own stirrings. Two years later she knew that God was calling her into overseas mission work as well. Certain of the call, Trudy and John told Jeannette and me. We asked them to wait before making the commitment—to be absolutely certain. But they said they had already waited, and they were sure. So they presented themselves to the Foreign Mission Board, now the International Mission Board of the Southern Baptist Convention, and John, who has a keen mind for business, was appointed treasurer of the missions in Brazil.

By that time, they had two beautiful children, Joy Kathryn and John IV. I had a hard time imagining my children and grandchildren 4,000 miles away in South America in unknown conditions totally different than the United States. The trip to the airport was one of the most difficult days of my life. I couldn't bear to watch the plane taxi away from the gate. I wondered if I would ever see them again.

While living in Rio de Jañeiro, Trudy had their third child, Angela Jeannette. Jeannette flew to Rio for Angela's birth, and we both went to Brazil later to visit. The situation was almost overwhelming. Our grandchildren were growing up in the streets of Rio and attending a church with a dirt floor. I asked Trudy and John if they thought this was the proper environment for their children to grow up in, and they insisted that they were where God wanted them. New churches were being established, including one that John was pastoring himself. When Jeannette and I came home, I was more troubled than ever.

Jeannette went down there again when David was born in

1987, but this time the delivery did not go smoothly. David was not breathing on his own initially. Jeannette called and said the next twenty-four hours would be critical. He might not make it. I knew I had to get to Brazil right away. David remained in ICU for the next twenty-one days.

Only three days after David's birth, Trudy began to have complications and required emergency surgery. I drove to the Brazilian consulate in Atlanta to get a visa, which is required for visiting Brazil. They told me it would take three or four days for them to process it, and my emotions almost overwhelmed me. I was unable to explain to the woman at the counter that Trudy was in pain and David was in grave danger. The woman remained calm and even remembered Jeannette from several days earlier. "She was in here and gave us a 'Be Our Guest' card," she said. "Did something happen to her?"

"No, it's my daughter," I said.

"Sit right here," the lady said.

In fifteen minutes she was back, visa in hand.

We find ourselves in the shadow of doubt—in the shadow of death sometimes—and the Lord's presence carries us through. That woman was an angel of mercy for me during an uncertain, frightening time.

When I arrived in Brazil, I began to see for the first time what held John and Trudy there. The Brazilian people loved them so much, and the missionaries were for them like an extended family. Trudy and David needed several transfusions, and the missionaries donated the needed blood. They also all prayed for Trudy and David. The Lord used this difficult situation to win my heart and give me peace about where they were. When I left Brazil, I knew they were where God wanted them.

They were transferred to Brasilia, the capital city of Brazil, and Jeannette and I visited them for two weeks after Christmas. They told us about the families they had come to know, and about the many children with special needs. I wanted to help.

"Why not build a foster home for Brazilian children like ours in the States?" I suggested. Land was inexpensive, and needy children were in abundance. John said he could find the land, and we moved forward. Trudy and John spread the word among the missionary families, and they identified a couple to serve as house parents. They were Brazilian but had lived for seven years in Canada and spoke English. They had one daughter, and had for years dreamed of working with foster children or orphans.

Jeannette and I were down there when the time came to select the first children for the foster home. We went to a small orphanage where nobody spoke English. I don't speak Portuguese either, so we communicated with smiles and hugs. I met a beautiful little boy, Michael, and we both felt a bond immediately. He sat in my lap and I rocked him. He seemed to trust me completely. When we left the orphanage, I asked if Michael could come live at our home, and he came with us right then.

We were there for several more days, and Michael and I spent many more hours together, laughing, playing, and rocking until he fell asleep. When it came time for Jeannette and me to return to the United States, Michael was crushed. He had been uprooted so many times in his life already—we both cried as they pried us apart.

Every year from that time on Jeannette and I went down for two weeks after Christmas. The foster home is thirty miles out from the city in the interior farmland. They have a farm where they grow some crops and raise cattle and, more important, take care of ten beautiful Brazilian children.

When we're there I ride with the children to school, hugging them all as they leave, then greet them with hugs in the afternoon. And even though I never learned Portuguese, they learned enough of my language for me to ask them, "Is everybody happy?

"Yeah, man, H-A-P-P-Y!"

CHAPTER SIXTEEN

A New Generation of Leadership

Jimmy Collins, our President and Chief Operating Officer, retired from Chick-fil-A in 2001 after thirty-three years of service. He announced his intentions five years earlier, then worked with my older son, Dan, preparing him to take over the position. Dan's brother, Bubba, continues as Senior Vice President.

I celebrated my eightieth birthday the same year. I still work more than a forty-hour week, but at some point in the future I will no longer play an active role in the company I founded. Dan, Bubba, and Trudy will take the responsibility for Chick-fil-A and the WinShape Centre Foundation and all its programs. Their complementary talents and interest hold the promise of a bright future.

Dan and Bubba, as you would expect from any two brothers, approach the operations differently. Dan's interest draws him to the processes—the business aspects of running the company. Bubba likes to spend more time with people. Dan and Bubba's

---

Above: Dan Cathy, left, serves as President and Chief Operating Officer, and Bubba, right, as Senior Vice President of Chick-fil-A.

mutual respect for each other and strong working relationship will allow them to make the best of the combination. Although Trudy does not participate in the day-to-day operation of Chick-fil-A, she speaks at many of the openings of new Chick-fil-A restaurants and other marketing related events. She and her husband, John, now live in Richmond, Virginia, and she continues to keep her hand directly on the foster home in Brazil that she and John founded.

Jeannette and I worked to prepare our children for the responsibility that will become theirs, and they likewise are preparing their children to become owners one day. Our twelve grandchildren, unlike Dan, Bubba, and Trudy, never had an opportunity to scrape gum from the underside of tables or sing to customers, but they're growing up in the atmosphere of Chick-fil-A. Dan and Bubba take their children on trips to visit Operators. Dan and his wife, Rhonda, also host training dinners for Operators in their home, as do Bubba and his wife, Cindy. The grandchildren are soaking in those experiences, learning the concepts and vocabulary of the business.

It's much more important, however, that they grow up to be responsible, godly adults, and our children have created the atmosphere for each of them to thrive.

Bubba and Cindy, with their home on a lake, have a basketball area and a big basement with a scaled-down version of Truett's Grill that attract kids by the dozens. Parents know their children will be visiting a safe home where there's no drinking and no open marital disputes. Trudy's children lived for ten years in Brazil as a missionary family, making them more sensitive to the needs of people around the world. They have a special heart for the Lord and for hurting children.

In January 2000, our children asked Jeannette and me to

meet with them for dinner at the Chick-fil-A headquarters. There they presented to us a covenant to each other and to us regarding our family and the future of the company, pledging:

We will be faithful to Christ's lordship in our lives. As committed Christians we will live a life of selfless devotion to His calling in our lives. We will prayerfully seek His leadership in all major decisions that impact our family and others. Our family roles as spouses to our lifelong mates, parents to our children, and loving aunts and uncles will be our priority. We will be accountable to each other to live a life of integrity following our parents' example of sacrifice, discipline, frugality, and service to others. We will model a work ethic we expect others to follow.

We will be faithful to carry on our family and corporate heritage. Because of our respect for our parents' commitment to touch peoples' lives in a unique way, we covenant to carry on the purpose and the mission of Chick-fil-A, WinShape Homes, and other related programs. Recognizing that our humanitarian and philanthropic interests are predicated on a strong and healthy business, we commit to operating Chick-fil-A restaurants with standards of excellence in our products, service, and cleanliness. The basic core philosophies and values with which we were raised, including our policy of being closed on Sunday, will be upheld and protected. Consistent with our past we will continue to provide opportunities for others by growing the business conservatively, moderating our growth and creating employment stability. We will fund the growth of Chick-fil-A with internally generated capital and debt rather than going to the public market. We will work to maintain the entrepreneurial spirit and professional development from our Chick-fil-A Operators and our corporate staff.

We covenant to work cooperatively with each other. In the spirit of humility and dependence on one another and to ensure consistence and unity, we will seek the advice of each other in making major decisions. We will pray for each other and trust God to give us the strength of character needed to fulfill our stewardship responsibilities.

Our children have committed to protecting and building upon what we have created, nurturing and caring for it, glorifying God, not seeking praise for themselves, and caring for the customer first.

Their challenge is also your challenge: to apply these principles in your life and your business, then to respond to the unexpected opportunities that will inevitably arise . . . to inspire other people.

Yesterday is history.
Tomorrow is unknown.
The present is God's present to us
to do with it as we choose.

Truett and his brother Ben grew up to be business partners at the Dwarf House restaurant.

Truett was drafted in the U.S. Army, where he served until he was discharged in 1945.

Bubba, Dan, and Trudy—with Jeannette's coaching—sang a jingle in the studio for a Dwarf House radio commercial.

Truett presented the First Lady, Lady Bird Johnson, with a Chick-fil-A Chicken Sandwich when she visited Georgia in 1964.

Former President Jimmy Carter greeted staff members on a visit to Chick-fil-A headquarters.

The history of Chick-fil-A is chronicled in a mural at many of the chain's restaurants.

The first Chick-fil-A billboard, featuring a huge 3-D rubber chicken, appeared in 1995. A few months later the Chick-fil-A Cows made their first appearance, and they've been making history ever since.

Truett's Grill, a 1950s-style diner, opened in 1996 to commemorate Truett's fifty years in the restaurant business.

Truett and Jeannette knew they had come to a special place when they visited the Mountain Campus at Berry College (above). That visit led to the creation of a unique partnership with the college that has allowed 780 students to attend Berry on WinShape scholarships.

The Cathys' dedication to scholarship is commemorated by a statue in downtown Atlanta signifying the awarding of $1,000 scholarships to Chick-fil-A team members. By 2002 the WinShape Foundation had provided scholarships to 16,500 students attending 2,030 colleges.

Truett and Jeannette (second row center) celebrate their children and grandchildren, the Whites, the Cathys, and the Faulks.

Truett travels in style, whether in a Cow car (right) or on his motorcycle (below).